Surviving the

Narcissist's Dance

Zac Thatcher

"Our greatest glory is not in never falling, but in rising every time we fall."

Confucius

Surviving the
Narcissist's
Dance

Zac Thatcher

DEDICATION

My story is written with the unconditional love my beautiful parents created for my siblings and myself. It is also written in acknowledgement of my much-loved children and the wonderful support they gave me during this difficult period of my life, as well as the hope that they will one day see me in the same light in which I will forever hold my own parents.

Contents

Preface

Surviving the Narcissist's Dance is my truth, thoughts, and opinions. It is written with the acknowledgement that I have no formal qualifications in mental health and psychology.

My story describes how I was deceived by a near-perfect chameleon-like act, and endured psychological, emotional, and on one occasion physical abuse, was discarded, spiralled down to the lowest point in my life, recovered, and moved on from a presumed narcissistic relationship.

My story describes the day-to-day madness of living within a presumed narcissistic relationship with a person you loved. It is not about revenge, bitterness, or causing hurt to anyone. It is also not about apportioning blame. After an intense period of healing and personal growth I am over the experience, have forgiven the main protagonist, and moved on with my life. Although I have come to terms with what happened, I doubt I will ever forget what I lived through.

My story is written for those who have realised that they are involved in a narcissistic relationship, those who are seeking to leave, those who are recovering, and those who have moved on. I am hoping it will also serve as a warning about the increasing number of narcissistic people in the community, seeking new 'sources of supply' in this increasingly 'all about me' world in which we live. It is my belief that narcissistic people are being produced by Western society with production-line efficiency.

As this is a book of my experiences, identity protection is very important to me. While it is important to me to tell my version of events as accurately as possible, it is also extremely important that I protect the identities of those involved in the experience.

Overview

I survived the narcissist's dance!

I wanted to make this statement at the beginning and the very end of this book. What lies in between is the story of how I was duped and drawn into a presumed narcissistic relationship.

I have finally got to the point where I have the confidence in myself to share my story in this book and most importantly the messages that it conveys. If it helps at least one person through the type of relationship I have lived, survived, and moved on from, then it is all well and good.

My second marriage, to a person I thought was very special, was more than a toxic relationship or marriage that simply did not work out. The reality was that I unknowingly married a presumed narcissist. If you marry a narcissistic person there is a high probability that the union will be more or less doomed before it even begins, and you are highly likely to pay a heavy personal and emotional price.

The failure of my second marriage affected me deeply. I felt new lows, and entertained all sorts of thoughts over a period of several months, before a strong sense of self kicked in and I managed to pull myself out of the downward spiral. I found my pain embarrassing to go through, as my issues seemed trivial compared to friends, family, and work colleagues around me going through battles with cancer and other illnesses, and seemingly coping much better with those traumas than I was with the breakdown of my relationship.

What helped me gather myself and move on? I have to thank my beautiful parents for the strong sense of self they gave me, and an upbringing with unconditional love which enabled me to keep going when things got tough. My siblings and their families also offered a quiet and confidential ear, as well as encouragement and support. I also had my beautiful children, from my first marriage, who were always wonderfully supportive and encouraging during my recovery phase, whilst being unaware of the finer details of what had taken place. I also had many wonderful friends and colleagues who gave their friendship, support and encouragement. All of these people helped me heal, along with the help of my insightful psychologist.

Before I commence my story, I will provide some background information, to set the scene and ensure the book unfolds as it should.

Why I Decided to Write this Book

I have always had a love of writing, but until this point in my life I did not have the confidence in myself, the subject matter, or the time to sit down and complete the process.

It was not cathartic for me to write my story. The message of my story is not about revenge but fairness. It is my strongest belief that people who have experienced narcissistic relationships need to be heard. Their stories need to be told so that others can learn and be warned.

In writing my story I accept a number of realities. There are always two versions of the truth. I believe that we are all on the same spectrum of human behaviours and characteristics. It is only the various degrees of behaviours and characteristics that differ for each of us. That is what makes us human and individual.

Everyone has a story to tell and we are all unique. Most, however, do not have the ability to tell their story in a written forum, or perhaps don't have the confidence to do so. No single story is greater than another's, with the message behind the story being what is most important.

The message of my story is not about labelling, directly attacking, or calling out the main protagonist, but to call out the destructive and extremely damaging actions and behaviours of narcissistic people. I believe my story to be of public interest. I also believe that the laws of defamation, or the veiled threat thereof, should not prevent these stories from coming out in the interest of the public and am comfortable suggesting that the laws of defamation around the world should be revised and updated for modern times, especially if a story is told with sensitivity to the people involved.

I believe my story is contemporary. It is interesting to note that current trends in society are recognising the damaging effects of coercive, controlling and manipulative actions and behaviours in relationships. Many governments are now looking to criminalise coercive control and the associated manipulative and abusive actions and behaviours in relationships due to the severe damage they can do to the recipient's sense of self-identity.

I am writing my story for all the other people in the world who have experienced a narcissistic relationship and who may be involved in one now. I am proud to publish my story, but more importantly for having the courage to tell my story and the messages it conveys. I hope it inspires others to avoid, leave, recover, and move on from narcissistic relationships.

I have come across a considerable amount of material about narcissistic relationships, and the majority seems to be written by women about men, or by health professionals who have not experienced a narcissistic relationship firsthand. This led me to wonder why there is so little written by men who have experienced the destructive outcomes that are often the result of a narcissistic relationship, because there are certainly many female narcissists who are involved in relationships in our society.

I have been lucky enough to have had a respectful relationship with my second wife's former partner, and after the breakdown of my marriage, it was a brief conversation with him that really kickstarted my recovery process, as I came to understand that we effectively lived the same experience with the same person. I am indebted to him for his assistance in helping me see that it was highly likely we were not the ones with the significant psychological and emotional issues, and associated complications.

While in no way taking away from the domestic violence that occurs against women by men, it is also important to me to raise awareness that domestic violence can be perpetrated by a woman against a man.

Introduction to Stella & Myself

For the purposes of identity protection, I will refer to my second wife as Stella, and not give the names of the children involved in our blended family.

My story is written with the understanding that no two people are the same. We all do things in our own way and interpret the same experiences within the context of our own lives. I have been involved in two failed marriages and I cannot put my hand on my heart and say that I am blameless. In this case, however, I accept that the chances of the marriage working long term were limited. My psychologist informed me that these types of relationships could be made to work, but the level of self-sacrifice and possible damage to your own self-concept and wellbeing is far beyond the norm of compromise.

Stella emigrated to a new country with her family at a relatively young age, and grew up in one of the newer suburbs of the city in which her family settled.

Not overly academic at school, she made the best of her abilities, enhanced by a bright and bubbly outward persona. With no formal tertiary qualifications she forged an outstanding corporate career, and is highly regarded by her employer.

Her memories of her childhood seem vastly different to those of her siblings, who seem to have dealt with their upbringings in a far more balanced way than Stella. She spoke about a number of things that shaped her way of thinking and contributed to the person she is today. Such as stories of how her brothers 'got the steak and she got the mincemeat.' Her male siblings were heavily supported by their parents in developing promising junior sporting careers, while she had to stay home and contribute towards the housekeeping duties, including ironing her father's shirts.

Stella told me of times her mother would beat her and throw her against walls. Birthdays and Christmas times were not fun, and presents were rare. To get away from all of this, Stella lived at her best friend's house for a considerable period of time from her mid-teens.

I never met Stella's father, but understand him to be a very chauvinistic and manipulative person. He would often pressure her to give him money, telling her stories of misfortune, which would play on her mind. If she chose not to give him money, then she would feel guilty and if she did give him money then she would feel manipulated. She always lived with a sense of trepidation, waiting for her father to ask for more money.

To the best of my knowledge, there was no incest or alcoholism in the family. I can well understand that it would not have been easy for her parents to move to another country from overseas, where they had lived through World War II, with young children, and needing to learn to speak another language, in order to establish themselves in a new country. Stella's father also lived with a significant medical issue.

Stella married in her early twenties, but the marriage only lasted a very short period of time before separation and divorce. She had bouts of post-natal depression after the birth of each of her children, spending a considerable amount of time on anti-depressants before returning to work on a full-time basis, so that her children were effectively raised in their early years by her former partner.

In terms of Stella's character and potential as a partner, a relatively minor issue was that she had cats, which was not ideal as one of my children was highly allergic to cats. However, before we moved in together, Stella agreed to sell her cats, which I think she did with a great deal of regret.

More significantly, I was aware that she had a troubled family background, and that she had been separated from her former partner for less than a year. A brief relationship had also taken place during this period.

Needless to say, I failed to take these red flags into account.

Stella's strategy for coping with these difficulties was to work extremely hard, at an almost frenetic level. She found it difficult to relax and was a perfectionist in all she did. I came to understand that she had also developed a scorecard mentality and a conditional mindset with regard to the way she lived.

She seemed preoccupied with how much she thought other people had done in a task. She had to beat that level of effort. Stella couldn't bear to see anyone outdo her level of effort and input. I heard Stella on a number of occasions verbalise questions such as, 'Why do I have to work so hard?' and, 'Why do other women have it easier than me?'

In terms of conditional thinking, she believed that by doing things for people she would earn their gratitude and love in return. This way of viewing the world was foreign to me, and bore no relation to the upbringing I had experienced.

With the benefit of hindsight, I have come to understand and accept that Stella's dysfunctional family background had led to her need for validation and admiration. Trust, belief, and giving others the benefit of the doubt – particularly with reference to her partner – were simply not things she was able to do. In her mind there was always an ulterior motive or some sort of underlying attempt at manipulation in everyone's actions and behaviours towards her. She always needed to prove that the warped thoughts she had about a person were real and true. However, when it came to her own actions and behaviours, she was hypersensitive to any criticism and, under any sort of personal pressure, had a victim mentality.

There always appeared to be a battle raging within Stella. It was as though she was always striving to justify herself to herself or make herself feel worthy. I think she knew she had significant emotional and psychological issues but chose to push them into the background and deflect them outwards, rather than facing up to her issues, seeking sustained professional help, and implementing the necessary changes. It was difficult and exhausting to watch this daily struggle. Emotionally, for the majority of the time, I felt as though I was dealing with a prepubescent child. This was in stark contrast to the highly regarded, consummate professional who operated in the corporate world.

Stella's upbringing, and the way she saw and interpreted her childhood, undoubtedly played a major part in her presumably developing Narcissistic Personality Disorder (NPD). Her need to over-compensate and exaggerate both the good and the bad in almost every aspect of her life seemed to be an attempt to rid herself of the bad memories, to feel worthy, and to come to terms with things. She was a deeply unhappy woman, looking for external factors, such as outstanding achievements in her workplace and praise from other people, to fill the void. She also suffered from significant anxiety issues that led to a plethora of minor, ongoing physical ailments.

Stella managed to expertly cover up these behaviours and traits before our wedding. If I had seen even a tiny percentage of the narcissistic actions and behaviours that she directed towards me once we were married, I would have walked away.

You tend to see yourself a little differently from the way those around you see you. However, I will do my best to give an objective view of who I am.

As mentioned previously, I have come to realise how lucky I was to grow up in a family environment of unconditional love. By unconditional love, I mean that I was given every opportunity to find my way in life, knowing that my parents were always there to provide support and encouragement in all that I decided to take on and do, and to pick up the pieces when things went wrong. There were no requirements placed upon me to receive their love and support, beyond the normal borders and boundaries associated with raising a child.

My father was employed in the public sector and my mother was primarily an excellent stay-at-home mother. I was a middle child, with both older and younger siblings. We did not have many of the trappings of life, but we did not seem to want for too much. We were able to enjoy time together during the extended holiday periods, which normally involved road trips to different destinations around the country we lived in.

Both my parents were strong people, firm but fair. I was occasionally smacked if I had been warned enough and did not listen. I was given responsibilities and accountabilities that were appropriate to my age.

I was educated at a variety of public schools, as my father moved around in his employment as a government employee. Even though I changed schools a number of times, I obtained a number of qualifications that held me in good stead in my area of employment.

I have had longstanding employment in a client-facing role. I enjoy helping clients deal with a whole range of personal and financial circumstances. The role has required me to be a good listener, and to be able to work out the difference between what people tell me is going on and what is *really* going on. The relevance of this information is that my career is founded on good listening and communication skills, as well as the ability to read body language and voice tone.

I cruised through my school years, putting in a minimum of effort to obtain reasonable academic results. My time was spent playing a wide variety of sports, which served as a great distraction from the more unwholesome activities that children and teenagers get up to. It also taught me invaluable lessons around the need to put team first in order to achieve success, rather than putting myself first. I experienced the emotions around winning and losing, doing my best but not always getting the desired result, and being resilient. I had a number of opportunities to advance with my sporting endeavours to more elite levels, but was always caught short with regard to putting in the effort that was required to give myself the chance of success. As I grew older self-discipline was sometimes an issue, as I fell for the attractions of the opposite sex, the pleasures of alcohol, and the use of social drugs.

I moved out of home at a relatively young age, straight into a home that I had bought with my own savings and a bank loan. Once out of home you tend to grow up far more quickly, as you have to be responsible for everything, from feeding yourself, to doing the housework, to paying the bills. I remember going back to my mother not long after leaving home, and thanking her for all she had done for me. The years in my unit were carefree, with a number of short-term and long-term relationships. Over this time I built on the solid sense of self that I had developed as a result of my stable, supportive upbringing and happy childhood.

I first married in my thirties. We had several children together, all of whom were still quite young at the point our marriage failed. The failure of my first marriage affected me deeply. I developed severe anxiety which can still be an issue under certain circumstances.

Parenting my children after the breakdown of my marriage was emotionally and financially challenging, but looking back they were also very rewarding times. I have to admit that I cannot put my hand on my heart and say that I am at all proud of the journey along which I have taken my children. I hope they come to see me as a loving father who did his best, and who was unconditional in his love for them.

I think my many and varied friends would describe me as being a little rough around the edges, although hopefully they would also add that I am intelligent, loyal, giving, sharing, often funny, sometimes serious, and keen to help others. In addition, they may point out that I can be very opinionated, prone to over-analysis, not overly politically correct, that I can struggle to let go, and I tend to wear my emotions on my sleeve.

I have to admit that I can get frustrated at times. I can also lose my cool and be a tad colourful in my actions and my language. While I see myself as being harmless, I am well aware of how these characteristics may appear to others, and they are not things I am proud of. I need to work on them on an ongoing basis.

Having given you the background to the circumstances and people involved, I would like to speak about the way in which the story will unfold. During the initial sessions with my psychologist we spoke about the 'over-evaluation phase', the 'devaluation phase' and the 'discard phase' of narcissistic relationships. My marriage to Stella, upon personal reflection and professional education on the matter, classically followed these three phases, and so the story will unfold along the same lines, although I am retitling the stages as the 'euphoria phase', the 'destruction phase', and the 'push the delete button phase.'

I am telling my story without too much background information about narcissistic relationships. I believe this will allow me to write with a relative degree of freedom and simply narrate what happened as I lived and experienced it.

Stage One:

The Euphoria Phase

The Beginning of the End

The euphoria phase of my relationship with Stella was exactly that – euphoric. The over-the-top feeling of euphoria should have been looked at by me as a big red flag, and I should have run away before any damage was done. Unfortunately, it didn't.

Once established in the relationship with Stella I came to realise that she was what is often referred to as a 'yummy mummy.' I first saw her at school one morning, taking her children to class. After the breakdown of my first marriage I would take my children to school early, and spend time with them kicking a football around on the asphalt. Within a short period of time, I had quite a number of children joining in the fun. One morning as I was about to kick the ball I saw Stella walking with her children. She was wearing a short pink mini dress with high black boots that stopped a couple of inches below her knees. I remember thinking that she could not possibly be a teacher, and went out on a wide ark to check out her figure. She looked sensational. Little did I realise then that she would become my second wife, and the subject of this book.

I first met Stella at a Saturday morning school sporting event. I had been out drinking the night before and was a little under the weather. We were playing a private school at their ground, and being from a little public primary school we wanted to make sure we put on a good performance. I was standing with my son, trying to figure out whether we were at the right spot, when Stella and her children came walking by. I could see that Stella's son had the primary school sporting outfit on under a jumper, and suggested we all stay together. The idea was for our sons to show their school sporting outfits, and hopefully everyone would then make their way towards us.

From there, we struck up an easy conversation talking about all sorts of things. I was not actually looking to 'pick her up', but the conversation seemed to lead down that path. I explained that I had several young children from my marriage. This was nearly always a conversation ender, but she didn't seem to be deterred by the fact. I then had to head down to the other end of the field to act as umpire.

While performing my umpiring duties I found myself looking at Stella from afar. I remember having an elevated heart beat and thinking that there was something going on here that was well out of the norm. At quarter time we both attended the huddle to hear the coach speak to the boys, and we kept glancing at each other while trying to make it look like we were not.

At a break in the game I decided to go for it with Stella. As the teams broke up to continue the game, I went up and gave her my business card with my mobile number written on it. I then said I would be interested in catching up with her but that I was not the chasing type, so I would leave it up to her to contact me. On the way back to continue my umpiring duties I rang my best mate and told him, 'I may have met my second wife.'

Stella later admitted that she, too, rang her best friend and told her that something weird had just happened, and that a guy had tried to pick her up at a school football match.

After the match the electricity between Stella and me was elevated, and I was keen to see if she would get in contact.

It was not until the following Wednesday that Stella sent me an email. I was then able to get her number, so that I could give her a call. I checked her out on Google, and saw that she was a professional woman, in quite a high position at the company she worked for. A professional woman, and someone who was financially independent, were things that were high up on my list. I had never had a relationship with a woman who was financially independent.

We spoke for hours on the telephone over the next week or so, getting to know each other better and enjoying each other's company.

On our first date we went out for a casual meal and a couple of drinks at a local pub. I picked her up from her place, and was slightly surprised to see another man in the house with her. He turned out to be one of her brothers, who was living with her to give her support after the breakdown of her former relationship. This was another red flag that I ignored.

Our relationship moved fast. Far too fast, in hindsight. Stella stayed over and the usual adult things happened. Everything seemed perfect and exciting, far more than anything that I had experienced at the very beginnings of a number of previous long-term relationships. Stella was everything I thought I was looking for in a life partner.

With the lengthy telephone calls continuing, we caught up as much as possible during the day for a quick chat and coffee, as we were both employed in the city centre. We had regular meals and even a week-long holiday with the children, which all went very well. These fun occasions gave me no indication of what was to come.

The reality is that Stella marketed herself to me in a very skilful fashion. She became what I wanted in every way. She was a very attractive hardworking business woman, financially independent, seemingly over her previous relationship, fun loving, broad minded, house proud, a wonderful cook and, most importantly, family orientated. I was completely taken in. With the benefit of hindsight, I was gripped by the 'family fantasy' that was unfolding in my mind.

After my marriage to Stella had failed, a close friend told me that Stella's former partner had revealed that Stella had said she would happily take him back, if things didn't work out with the woman he was seeing at the time. This was during the early, euphoric phase of my relationship with Stella. Her former partner declined her offer, telling her that they were very different people, and he had no interest in entertaining the thought.

I was also told that Stella's former partner had wanted to warn me about the woman I was rapidly falling in love with. He said that he thought I was a trophy husband for Stella. I was apparently a big step up from him in terms of status, earnings, and the ability to keep Stella in the manner to which she had clearly decided she could become accustomed.

I have absolutely no doubt that Stella's next relationship will be another big step up, possibly with a celebrity or someone who has significant wealth. The people she has left behind understand what lies ahead for him.

You may wonder if I ever asked myself why such an attractive woman with so much going for her was on the market in the first place. In truth, I did ask myself this question, and then proceeded to ignore the obvious red flags. Not only this, the period of time that I knew her before our marriage was far too short.

Within a few weeks of meeting Stella I booked a short holiday for two nights at a five-star wilderness resort, not far from where we lived. The cost was outrageous, but the destination was amazing and a fantastic experience. We both thoroughly enjoyed ourselves, and the relationship continued to develop at an ever-increasing rate. In keeping with our rapidly developing relationship theme within a couple of months we had discussed our finances and were looking at properties to buy, with a view to moving in together with our children. This was obviously a reckless and crazy thing to do. I remember during this time experiencing conflict with regard to my decision-making. Another red flag missed.

One particular house I remember inspecting with Stella was in the hills. It had some acreage, but was not too far from suburbia. We attended the open inspection and were both pretty happy with what we saw. We discussed how all the children would fit into the place, the level of affordability, our earnings, the value of our current homes, and the size of the mortgage. It was pretty heady stuff. The acreage was beautiful, the views were spectacular, it was easily affordable, the lifestyle looked very appealing, and it all came down to making a commitment or not. We walked into a little glade of pine trees on the property so we could both gather our thoughts. I said to Stella that if two particular species of bird came and sat in the pine trees and started singing that we should take it as a sign and put an offer in for the property then and there. Unbelievably, within a minute or so, the two birds did come and sit in the pine trees and started singing. Thankfully, that was too much for both of us. We decided to leave, feeling stunned and bewildered.

The difficulty with Stella having cats and one of my children having an allergy to cats was dealt with by her agreeing to sell them before we moved in together. With the benefit of hindsight, I could have handled this better, as both Stella and her children were much attached to their pets, as well as animal lovers in general.

On the flip side, I was skilfully kept away from Stella's family, apart from her siblings, while our relationship was in the euphoria phase. From memory, I met her mother at our first Christmas together in our new house. She had a very strong demeanour, was beautifully dressed, with a presence that commanded those around her to pay attention to her. Another red flag ignored.

During the euphoria stage there is only one incident that I can clearly recall where I had doubts about Stella's personality.

This incident occurred at my home, prior to the purchase of the house we bought together. It was a simple night in with a couple of friends. We had a light meal, listened to some music, and chatted away while enjoying a few wines. The more Stella drank, the more her demeanour changed. She made a number of slightly nasty and unnecessary comments, mostly directed at me, with a few directed towards our friends. These comments were ill considered, unguarded, arrogant, and somewhat aloof.

I dismissed her behaviour, as the good in our relationship was far outweighing the bad at that stage. I put it down to a combination of stress at work and too much to drink. In reality it was a mild taste of what was to come.

The house Stella and I purchased was a beautiful two-storey, resort-style place with plenty of space, a lovely swimming pool, and well-tended gardens. There was plenty of room for us and all the children, although the limited number of bedrooms meant that two of our younger children were placed in together in one bedroom. Initially, they both seemed to enjoy and appreciate this arrangement. The home was in a peaceful suburb not all that far from the city, and close to both our former partners' homes. The neighbours were great, and all seemed perfect.

To finance the new home I sold my house, cleared a small debt, and purchased a new car that would accommodate our combined family. Stella contributed her investment from the sale of her house. Before moving in she had free rein to paint the interior of the home as she wanted, and this was done with her usual enthusiasm and attention to detail.

From the outside looking in we must have seemed like the perfect family. We had good incomes, which supported a very comfortable lifestyle, the house was beautiful, there were fun-filled family holidays, and the children all got along well. I could not have been happier, and looked forward to all that I thought was going to be on offer as our relationship and commitment to each other strengthened and grew. The potential seemed unlimited.

Everyone quickly settled into the house, creating new routines, and looking forward to spending our first Christmas together. Our boys, in particular, were having a great time together riding their bikes, skateboarding, and playing cricket and football on the front lawn with their newly found neighbourhood friends. Fun times in the pool were also had, and enjoyed with friends and neighbours alike.

That first Christmas was an extravaganza. I soon learnt that Stella did not do things by half. Besides both immediate families being present there were a number of other relations, as well as a friend of mine and his two children.

The place was decked out with decorations, Christmas music was played, menus were printed, and the food was better than restaurant standard. It seemed as though hundreds of presents were placed around the beautifully trimmed tree.

Stella spent hours wrapping the many presents that I quite honestly thought were over the top in number. Christmas stockings were filled for each of our children and hung on the staircase to be found by them in the morning. In hindsight this was all clearly over-compensation for the lack of happy Christmases that Stella had experienced in her childhood.

Every aspect of the proceedings was photographed and placed on Facebook by Stella for everyone to see how great it all looked. Christmas was really important to Stella, and I happily played my part. My duties included cooking the massive turkey in our Weber barbecue, preparing the fish course, mixing and serving the drinks, and ensuring that the yard and pool were up to standard. Our Christmases took a lot of time and effort, and came with a price tag that ran into thousands of dollars.

Nevertheless, I was happy to go along with the Stella-style Christmases. I could see it was important to her, and made her feel good about herself.

However, in spite of all the effort that went into these festivities, with the benefit of hindsight, many of the people who attended didn't find them terribly festive. From the outside looking in, everything felt a little pressured and tight. It all seemed to be about putting on a display.

It wasn't until our first Christmas that I met Stella's mother. It was not an easy first meeting, and I noted the tension between the two of them. It was very noticeable on that day, and on every subsequent occasion throughout our time together. It seemed to be a very manufactured relationship.

However, overall, I thought our first Christmas together went really well. The food was fantastic, the environment appeared happy, and the occasion was certainly memorable.

The day began with me giving Stella her present and wishing her a 'Merry Christmas.' I was shocked after the breakdown of our marriage when she screamed, 'You didn't even hug me on our first Christmas.'

After the first Christmas we began establishing our new household. Time was spent with our relatives and friends, introducing everyone to each other, and settling down into the routines of family life. I noted that Stella had only one close friend, whom she had known since her schooldays.

I supported Stella in her blossoming career, attending functions and events as her partner. I was used to these occasions from my own career, and easily fitted into the role, mixing with the businesspeople with whom Stella was associating. They were good times, but lacked a sense of reality. It wasn't that I didn't enjoy this networking, but it was something I would have preferred to undertake on a less frequent basis. Stella, on the other hand, thrived on this type of corporate activity. It made her feel alive, special, and important, and maybe even as though she was part of the elite. It was all a little sycophantic for me.

Beyond the corporate networking, family fun times and holidays were also planned and enjoyed by all of us. I really believed that I had met a very special person, a lifelong partner with whom I had the opportunity to create a family that would last the journey.

Teething issues occurred for both of us with each other's children and how to best manage them, particularly in the area of how to deal with difficult behaviours. This was all normal and to be expected, with the different parenting that Stella and I experienced in our childhoods.

It seemed as though she felt the need to have more than others in order to feel good about herself. Pulling her weight, and even punching above her weight, were expected in her childhood as far as household duties were concerned. Idleness was met with physical consequences, and she grew up in an environment with conditional thinking and a scorecard mentality.

While we had a regular cleaner to assist, Stella put a list of duties up on the refrigerator for all the children, which was sometimes adhered to but on most occasions not. In particular she wanted my children to keep their rooms a lot tidier and to cook more. I had the philosophy of talking with my children and trying to get them to see the need to be responsible in assisting with the running of the home and learning the skills they would need when they finally moved to their own places. Physical consequences were obviously not an option, and the idea of taking things from the girls as a form of punishment was not appropriate for their ages. The boys, being a little younger, were different.

Stella's greatest problem with my children was the fact that I had more than she did. I also had challenges with her young children. Early on they tested me with some difficult behaviour and questioned my right to request something of them or to discipline them in an appropriate way for today's standards and expectations. On one occasion they told me I was not their father.

This type of problem with her children was sorted out fairly quickly and I explained to them that, although I was not their father, I was not going to put up with their bad behaviour towards me and, in particular, towards their mother. From there what happened would be up to them. In the end I had a solid relationship with Stella's children, which developed over time into a fulfilling bond that I still miss today. Stella's children were treated, protected, respected, and valued like my own.

I concede it would have been a confusing and difficult time for relatively young children, with their mother and father separating, and their mother becoming involved with me and my children, living in a new home, and effectively becoming a 'Brady Bunch', as well as the breakdown of the relationship between their father and mother. These were all fairly traumatic experiences for young children to go through, and on top of all this their father's new partner also had a young child, who Stella's children lived with for some time. None of this would have been easy to deal with for anyone, let alone such young children.

I also concede that it is also not easy to blend two families. Disciplining another person's children and knowing the borders and boundaries around this issue is an understanding that has to get sorted, often through a process of trial and error.

With the above in mind, I found some of Stella's behaviours and interactions with her children somewhat challenging. Her children just walking into our ensuite whenever they felt like it was one of these contentious issues. To me, our ensuite was our area and effectively should have been a children-free zone, within reason. Showering with her children I also found a little strange. Her children were well above primary school entrance age, and I suppose I had been brought up completely differently with regard to the appropriateness of this type of interaction between a mother and her children. Stella more or less ignored what I said on these matters, and passed it all off as me being too conservative. I got the feeling her children saw it as some sort of a victory for them in the household, which I did not think was healthy for all concerned.

Another issue that I struggled with concerning Stella and her children was the interaction between them when they returned from their father's. Her children were under a fifty/fifty shared parenting arrangement at the time and, having been involved in the same sort of arrangement with my first wife and my children, I understood her desire to see them again, as well as the anxiety you can get with separation from your children. Having mentioned this, I found the interaction between Stella and her children to be over the top. I honestly felt like the third wheel as they kissed on the lips numerous times, obviously not in a passionate and adult way, and hugged each other for an extended period of time as I sat on the couch amongst all of this. I used to think of it as being like a 'love fest.' I remember one of her children, on one occasion as they were hugging their mother, looking at me and pulling a face as if to say 'look what I have got and you haven't! I am in the position of power and control!' The need for all this was a little strange to me. It felt like overcompensation. A number of my family members and mutual friends expressed the same views with regard to the intensity of the interactions between Stella and her children. From her children's viewpoint, it was what they were used to, lived with, and were taught was normal. Stella's children also seemed to intuitively know that if they went along with these types of learned behaviours, everything would be easier and turn out for the best for them.

Perhaps the above interactions were something that I should have paid more attention to at the time, but I simply let them go as being the way Stella and her children did things. My thoughts with regard to these interactions also had to be tempered by the fact that she also had her own criticisms of my interactions with my children. Parenting styles can be a difficult area to work through, and often there is no clear right or wrong way of doing things.

From here, our relationship continued to move on at a rather rapid rate. There were numerous corporate outings, lovely family holidays, and enjoyable date nights. I could not have been happier.

With the positives far outweighing the negatives and no reason to doubt my decision, I proposed to Stella in the formal lounge room of our new home, a relatively short amount of time after having first met her. It was a spur of the moment thing, without the usual fanfare. When Stella said 'Yes' I felt like a million dollars, and we set about planning our wedding for later that year.

Asking Stella to marry me was done more for Stella than it was for me. I didn't think I would marry again and would have been happy to stay in a de facto relationship, given the outcomes are similar to a marriage if it all breaks down. I asked Stella to marry me to fulfil one of her needs, as her former partner had not asked Stella to marry him throughout their lengthy relationship. No dispersions are being cast on her former partner here. He had his own reasons for not asking Stella to marry him, and I understand all that more fully now having been involved in a failed marriage with Stella.

The build up to our wedding day was a mixture of hard work and excitement. We decided that we would marry in our backyard and hold our reception in an upmarket restaurant in the suburbs of the city in which we lived. Our backyard was a beautiful location for a simple, yet formal, wedding ceremony. The restaurant could accommodate the number of guests we wanted, could be booked out for the night and was happy to accommodate Stella's desire to theme the place in the colours that she wanted. The cost was more than reasonable and, based on previous dining experiences we'd had at the restaurant, the food and service were outstanding. I was really happy with the choices we had made together, and looking forward to our special day. From there, Stella set about getting everything organised in her very thorough and capable way. My job was to make the yard look presentable, and to organise drinks on the day. Getting the yard presentable took about six weeks for me to achieve, and was exhausting. There was lawn mowing to be done, fertilising, weeding, the pool had to be brought up to a pristine standard, painting undertaken, and pressure cleaning of the pavers.

We also decided to hold a number of dinner parties before the wedding, with a mix of our current mutual friends and those from our previous relationships, in order to help make our wedding reception an easy and fun night. I enjoyed these occasions. Stella was a great host and presented beautiful meals. The evenings seemed to go over very well, with interesting and engaged conversations going on and good quality wines enjoyed.

On one of these occasions Stella asked two couples over who had been friends of both herself and her former partner. I thought these nights also went well. Over time I noticed that these couples did not stay on as part of Stella's new life with me, and returned to their longstanding relationship with her former partner. A mutual friend later mentioned that they had felt difficult being involved with Stella, out of an understandable loyalty to her former partner, and had asked his approval to attend both the dinner parties as well as our wedding. Perhaps another red flag missed by me.

Once our marriage ended, so did Stella's friendships with our mutual friends.

The Wedding Day

Our wedding day was one of the happiest days of my life. I thought I was a very lucky man to be marrying Stella, and I had no doubts about my decision. As far as I was concerned it was beautiful and went extremely well. I thoroughly enjoyed myself, and was proud to be marrying Stella in front of our children, families, and friends.

Stella spent the night prior to our wedding with her best friend and her children, in the upmarket city hotel where we were also going to spend our wedding night. From the wedding pictures of the morning of our wedding, every stage of her preparation seemed to be photographed as she prepared for her big moment. There seemed to be hundreds of pictures of her makeup being meticulously applied, her dress, shots with her children, views from the hotel, and getting into and out of the limousine. Stella was most certainly the centre of attention on the day, and had a complete fuss made of her by all concerned.

I spent the night prior to our wedding day at our matrimonial home, swimming with a couple of mates and having a beer or two. It was an enjoyable and laid-back occasion. That night I was woken by a fairly severe storm, and went downstairs to see a torrent of rain pouring off the sails onto the pavers where our guests would be standing during our wedding ceremony. The weather forecast was not overly promising for the wedding day, so I set about trying to put a solution in place to make the area more waterproof, as well as creating a Plan B, should the weather at the crucial moment take a turn for the worse. This all occurred from about 2am until around 6am, so I didn't get much sleep.

On the wedding day, I remember working right up until our guests started to arrive. The weather remained a concern, but I also had to try and carry out some last minute instructions given to me by Stella.

A railing had to be strategically placed with red rope through it, so that she could walk amongst our guests in an uninterrupted fashion. A number of classy looking wooden candelabras with lighted candles had to be placed about the courtyard. I had trouble lighting all the candles, as it was too windy, so I gave that task away.

With guests starting to arrive, the people serving drinks in place, and nothing more that I could do, I raced upstairs to change. I had a quick shower and dried myself, but started to profusely sweat. I had a couple of shirts, as I had thought I would have this little problem. The nerves had started to set in. The first time I went downstairs to join our guests the sweating became so pronounced that I decided to quickly go back upstairs, have a second shower and present myself again, wearing the spare shirt. From there, I seemed to settle down and although being the centre of attention is not my forte, I enjoyed greeting everyone before taking my place with our celebrant. All I had to do now was to await Stella's arrival.

Stella arrived in a beautiful black limousine, accompanied by her mother and young children. Pictures were taken outside, and she then made her way down the side of the house to where our ceremony was to be held. First down the side was Stella's mother, beautifully dressed, as always, followed by the children and then the bride. There was a fantastic picture taken of Stella's children, one of my favourites of them, as they came into the patio area and saw all the guests. It was a picture that captured very purely their childlike sense of amazement, surprise, and sheer joy as they were greeted with cheers from the guests, and saw our beautiful backyard.

Finally, Stella came into view. She looked absolutely stunning. I was fairly happy at this stage that the celebrant's microphone was on mute, as I remember muttering an expletive.

From there, the marriage ceremony became a little bit of a blur for me. My children, Stella's children, and her best friend's child were all part of the ceremony. My parents and Stella's mother were all present. Family, friends, and neighbours filled the patio as we exchanged our personally written vows, and one of my poems was read out by the celebrant. I really enjoyed the moment. It was a beautiful location, setup, and ceremony. I felt very lucky and happy.

After the ceremony and the signing of the marriage certificate we mingled amongst the guests before having pictures taken. Our guests enjoyed themselves, with some lovely finger food and plenty of good quality champagne, wines, and a range of beers.

The guests departed an hour or so after the ceremony, and we left to have more wedding photos taken, and to travel to our reception. I now know that a number of people at our wedding ceremony believed it was highly likely that I was making a big mistake by marrying Stella. These people included colleagues from work, a couple of friends, a musician we had playing at the wedding, as well as two or three couples who were friends of Stella and her former partner. A colleague of mine mentioned to me after our separation that when Stella's mother walked into the patio area before the wedding he said to another work colleague that he thought I was going to be in trouble early, and it was destined not to work out all that well. He based that comment on the demeanour of Stella's mother as she walked through the patio area – it was almost as if the occasion and gathering was about her and her only.

A friend of Stella's signed our marriage certificate. I remember looking at this person just after the ceremony and the signing, and they seemed to have a rather strained look on their face. I think they knew what I was in for. After all, they had seen or heard it all before from Stella's former partner and, I suspect, from Stella's first husband.

A very talented guitarist was booked for our wedding. They had worked with Stella at a previous place of employment, and played wonderful acoustic versions of songs that were easy and pleasant to listen to. I spoke to the guitarist some years after our wedding, when they played at another wedding, and got the feeling that they sensed the difficulty that my marriage to Stella was going through. They told me that they'd had a heated exchange with Stella about her approach to life, her values, and the importance of being comfortable with yourself. I think it all ended with an agreement to disagree.

Having completed the final wedding pictures, Stella and I made our way to the reception, which I felt went very well. The speeches, by both Stella and myself, were well received.

One memory I do have is of a niece of Stella's deciding not to come to our wedding, which made for a very obvious empty seat at our table. Perhaps I should have read a lot more into her decision not to attend than I did at the time.

One of the highlights of my speech was to single out Stella's children and, in front of our guests, said, 'Just because I have married your mother it does not mean that your mum will not still be your mother and your dad still your father. You will all be looked after and supported as my own in my care, and if you want me to, I look forward to you all playing a significant part in my life, as well as you playing a significant part in my life, as stepfather and stepchildren.'

Before ending my thoughts on our reception, I have to mention the content of the conversation I had with a friend at the bar. Their comments at the time appeared to be right out of line, but proved to be 100% correct and very insightful. I was standing on my own enjoying a quiet moment and watching what was going on when this person came up to me and said, 'Congratulations on your marriage to Stella. She looks very beautiful tonight, as she usually does. I have known Stella for a long time now, and she is a person who can be false and fake at times, and I think does not really know herself.' You can imagine how shocked I was to hear these comments. Even taking into account that this person was quite drunk, I was stuck for words. We parted ways fairly quickly after the comments were made, and I remained stunned. It was difficult to understand why someone would say something like that, let alone at a wedding reception. In hindsight, they were perfectly correct in what they said. More honest words could not have been spoken. The words immediately lodged, somewhat uncomfortably, in my memory bank. Up until then I had not seen any evidence of any significance that justified what this person had said to me.

Having completed the cutting of the cake, we both decided it was time to leave our reception and head to the hotel. It had been a long and exhausting day for both of us.

This part of the evening had the potential to be a little difficult, with her children being capable of putting on what I will call a 'separation performance' from their mother. Before the wedding day I had spoken to Stella's children about how the day was their mother's and not theirs, and that they should be respectful of this and not spoil the day. Plans

A, B, and C were put in place to ensure any behavioural issues were dealt with and, to their credit, they behaved pretty well.

Once Stella and I had made our way through the tunnel of well-wishing wedding guests I made my way to the limousine and waited as she said goodbye to her children, in a rather extended fashion for one night only. Stella was eventually encouraged to leave by a relative, who took charge of her children and had them spend the night at her place with one of my children. They were, of course, fine. My mother later admitted to me that she thought the departure of Stella from her children was over the top, and mentioned that my aunty said words to the same effect.

With both of us finally in the limousine, we headed off to the city hotel where we were to spend our wedding night. As we drove I remember feeling incredibly tired but also very happy that all had appeared to go very well. Arriving at the hotel we left the limousine and walked through the lobby to the lifts to make our way to our room. Everyone in the hotel lobby stared admiringly at Stella as she walked to the lifts. She looked simply stunning. I was feeling both pretty proud of my wife, and believed I was a very lucky man.

Once at our hotel room I opened the door and Stella walked in ahead of me. I was looking forward to spending a relaxing, quiet, and romantic evening with my wife. How wrong I was.

I ran the spa and suggested to Stella that we jump in and enjoy a wine or two, or perhaps a glass of champagne. After the spa we jumped into bed and the usual things happened, but I had a sense that Stella was not at all happy. I have to admit that I am not the world's most romantic man, but do not feel that I am a total fool in the area of romance. Here is what I was told by Stella after our separation. She expected me to carry her into our wedding room. I was then expected to disrobe her item by item, noticing the henna tattoo she had placed on her body and, I suppose, make passionate love to her all night. I failed to give her the fairytale wedding night she wanted. I was a very poor mind reader. I did not mean to hurt her feelings or fail to fulfil her needs and expectations for our wedding night. Looking back on it all, our wedding night had little chance for success. Stella's extreme level of disappointment, and the intent she attached to me for deliberately making it that way are borne out by two things Stella said after we separated, 'You didn't even carry me into the room on the wedding night', and, 'You married a broken person who didn't really emotionally commit to the marriage.'

This first statement was made in anger, as Stella carried bitterness towards me for 'intentionally' hurting her feelings on our wedding night in such a catastrophic way. The second statement I will discuss later in the book. At this stage, all I will say is that I believe Stella married for reasons other than genuine love and commitment. It is rather ironic that my mother, after the separation, mentioned that before our wedding Stella had said to her that in meeting me she had met her soulmate.

There I was on our wedding night thinking what a great decision I had made and how good and exciting the future was going to be. I honestly thought I had married a much better person than my first wife – physically attractive, professional, financially independent, a go-getter, hardworking, broad minded, fun loving, house proud, family orientated, and someone who valued my children and was prepared to play a significant role in their lives. Stella also appeared to have separated from her former partner in a decent way, with the financial split, shared parenting arrangements, and child maintenance payments all sorted in a relatively quick period.

Someone mentioned to me, after our separation, this had only happened because her former partner conceded on most points, and the settlement of all issues was in Stella's favour.

The reality is that our wedding night clearly and distinctly marked the end of the Euphoria Phase, and the beginning of the Destruction Phase of our relationship and marriage.

I had no idea whatsoever as to what I had got myself into, or what lay ahead.

The Morning After & The Honeymoon

I now think our wedding night also marked the peak of our relationship. I rapidly fell from being described by Stella as her soulmate, and being told that I was funny, clever, insightful, irreverent, handsome, caring, a great dad, passionate, interesting, and deep.

The morning after the wedding, following a nice breakfast at our hotel, we headed back home. Two of my children greeted us, along with some of their cousins and my father, who had stayed the night to look after the children. My two children, in a gesture I will always remember, had made a large heart on the kitchen bench top out of little red heart-shaped sequins that contained the words 'Dad and Stella 4 Ever.' I thought it was very touching and something that they did not have to do, but which showed they were on board with the marriage, and excited by what lay ahead.

That day, my children went back to their mother, and Stella's to their father, and we packed our bags for the honeymoon. The destination was a wilderness retreat, about a day's travel and a couple of plane flights from where we lived.

It was on our honeymoon that I began to further sense that something had most definitely changed between us. These feelings were confirmed by a number of comments Stella made, as well as issues she raised that were new to me. The first thing was that she did not really like the place. I must admit I was a little disappointed as well, but was more than happy to be with my new bride on our honeymoon. The retreat had very well-appointed cabins, situated at various locations around the main dining and lounge areas. To get to these areas you had to walk through the bush on raised wooden pathways in the exposed weather. It was not that much of a big deal, and I encouraged Stella to make the most of it. It could have been much worse.

It was on the honeymoon that I started to notice some disparaging comments that Stella made towards me, that I had not really noticed before. These comments included her not being happy with my clothing choice, eating or drinking too much, as well as not being able to keep up with her when we went on a nature walk. The fact that I had a rather arthritic knee from years of playing sport and simply getting older, suddenly became an issue. I enjoyed walking but needed to be careful of my steps, especially going downhill. However, I could still walk at a reasonable pace. Stella's comments bordered on being hurtful, unhelpful, and simply not necessary. They were a precursor to many more such comments to come.

The biggest issue on the honeymoon was my unbearable snoring, an issue that I cannot remember being raised before. I awoke after the first morning to find I was alone in bed, and that Stella had seen fit to spend most of the night trying to sleep on couch cushions, down the hallway of our cabin. She seemed to have got very little sleep and was distressed and agitated. I was really confused by all of this, as it had not been an issue, at all, from the time I had met her until the first night of our honeymoon.

All in all, I enjoyed our honeymoon and returned home still very optimistic about our future together, and completely oblivious to what had started to unfold.

Stage Two:
The Destruction Phase

The Cracks in The Wall

From this point forward, I noticed a rapid increase in issues being raised by Stella that had not been issues in the past. I initially put these little problems down to teething issues, and hoped that things would settle down with the passing of time. We had, after all, been living with each other for a reasonable period of time before the wedding without too much difficulty.

Before going too much further I want to spend some time describing some of Stella's character traits and issues that emerged once we had married. These descriptions will give context to what it was like to live with her, before I describe in some detail the many unfortunate incidents I experienced with Stella throughout our marriage. These will include comment on things I called The Walls, Conditional Thinking, Scorecard Mentality, Stella Facts and Hoops, Love Tanks, Stella the Perfectionist, Stella's Control Freak Mentality, Always Comparing Other Relationships to Ours, Pleading the Fifth, the Split Between Household Duties, My Understanding of Stella's Perception of Love, and The Vault of Resentment. Many of these things became evident when we were alone together. They were skilfully covered up by Stella when our children, relatives, friends, or work colleagues were around.

I also need to spend some time describing an incident that occurred at her mother's home one evening, as well as describing the tantrums, emotional meltdowns, and tirades that Stella regularly directed towards me.

Before elaborating further, I also want to say that there were a number of good times experienced with Stella and our family that I will always appreciate with regard to the role she played.

What follows is not an attempt to pull someone apart or seek to completely assassinate their character. It is simply my view of what I was trying to live with, juggle, and sort my way through on a daily basis, as I also dealt with my own range of day-to-day work and life pressures.

* * *

I think we all have walls that we put up around ourselves as we grow and react to the life experiences that come our way. These walls are about being cautious and protecting our sense of self, sense of worth, and self-concept. Most of us want to be loved, and accept that we have to let our walls down to a special person if we want to take part in the full experience that real love has to offer. The price you pay, if it doesn't work out, can obviously be extremely emotionally painful, with the effects lasting for many years. However, I believe in the old saying that it is better to have loved and lost than never to have loved at all.

Stella's walls—aka The Walls—were not a problem in the courtship phase, but sprung up after we married and were impenetrable from that point forward. I spent my entire marriage to Stella battling with this problem. It seemed that once she married me she simply checked out emotionally. I have to admit that I was completely taken in by the display that Stella put on during the courtship phase of our relationship. With the benefit of hindsight, it would be safe to say that she was never emotionally committed to our relationship.

My married years with Stella were spent trying to feel her emotional presence in our relationship. Metaphorically I tried climbing over, digging under, coming from both sides, entering through the doors and windows. I tried tough love, soft love, pandering to her, and attempting to give her what I thought she wanted. I tried talking to her, writing to her, and gently suggesting that she needed some professional help, which I was willing to participate in, as it was obviously proving to be very damaging to our relationship. I will write more about the professional help Stella did eventually seek, and the extent of the professional help she'd had in her past, which she watered down.

In the end all measures and attempts to deal with Stella's walls were to no avail. It was frustrating and hurtful, as I knew that it was up to her to deal with her issues. Put simply, Stella's walls could be dismantled very quickly if she wanted them to be. The problem and the solution lay with her. For Stella's walls to go, it had to be an inside job with support from outside influences. Throughout the entire marriage, Stella's walls only came down three or four times. What I saw when this did happen was a very vulnerable person, a little girl in her emotional development, and someone who did not appear to have a good sense of self. It was all very sad to see, but it seemed fixable, with help and Stella's desire to tackle the problem. I also saw the very beautiful person I now understand and accept acted out in the courtship phase of our relationship. It appeared to me, at the time, that the Stella I saw in the courtship phase of our relationship was the person she wanted to be. I have no doubt that the beautiful person I saw when Stella's walls came down briefly was the person she could be, if she only faced up to her issues.

One of the very few times when Stella's walls came down happened on an occasion when all our children were with us, and Stella had cooked one of her wonderful evening meals. I remember we were all sitting on the couch, which was always a little cosy with all of us sitting on it at the same time, watching TV, chatting away, and enjoying our meals. Both Stella and I had finished our meals and I remember her putting her arm around me and looking at me with one of those looks that gives you a peep into someone's soul. What I saw was the beautiful person I know Stella could be if she just thought better of herself. I also saw that vulnerable little girl whose dysfunctional emotional state had stayed with her into adulthood.

I quietly said, with the children all around, 'You just let me in, didn't you? It was beautiful, thank you for doing that.'

With those words Stella's walls went straight back up, and I saw the window to her inner self slam shut in front of me.

Conditional Thinking

Conditional thinking in a personal relationship is something that is most unusual to me. I understand this way of thinking in the corporate world, where Stella excels, but not as something that would create an environment for success in a personal relationship. In saying this, I understand and accept that we all do things for one another within relationships with the aim of pleasing the other and wanting to make our special person feel appreciated and special. However, Stella wanted more than this as an outcome.

The corporate world is full of conditional thinking. If you do your work well you are rewarded by keeping your job and receiving wages, being recognised with bonuses or gifts, and having the possibility of promotion. Outcomes are often planned and worked towards, with the end result of something you want in mind and incentives on offer. We all have a work face and a private face, and know how to play the game in a professional context. I felt that Stella employed business strategies in her personal relationships by attempting to manage the relationship and produce an outcome that was shallow, emotionally false, and lacking in any sincerity or depth.

In a personal relationship, if you employ conditional thinking, then you are not doing things for others for the right reasons. Doing things for your special person and expecting gratitude or praise in return, beyond the norm of a simple thank you as a sign of appreciation, is to enter into a business transaction. Effectively, you are not doing things for yourself, or others, for the satisfaction that comes from giving, but entering into a transaction with the expectation of gaining something in return. This is not true love.

In my view, random acts of kindness should be spontaneous, cost little, and promise no rewards.

Keeping a Scorecard

Stella was very preoccupied with how much other people, in particular her partner, had undertaken or achieved, in comparison to her. Stella always had to see herself as having done more, or to have beaten the level of effort she thought the other person may have put in.

Living with this type of thinking and mentality was destructive, negative and very disheartening. With this type of thinking, the fair division of housework and household duties, as far as Stella was concerned, was a never-ending issue. Suffice to say, she always thought she did far more than me when it came to household duties. In reality this was simply not the case.

On one occasion, when completely frustrated by Stella's scorecard mentality, I asked her to sit down so that I could demonstrate how this type of thinking was making me feel.

I drew a T bar at the top of a piece of paper, with Stella's name on the left and mine on the right. I then asked Stella to tell me all the things she had done that day. There would have been things like multiple loads of laundry, cooking, some light housework, and grocery shopping for Stella. On my side of the ledger there may have been gardening, watering, cleaning the pool, lawn mowing, and perhaps stacking or unstacking the dishwasher.

I then attached an imaginary score to each task and added things up for both of us. Naturally, I added things up so that I came out on top to the fifth decimal point. I then somewhat sarcastically asked Stella what all this meant. I said that it all meant nothing in my opinion, and that I was not happy to live with this type of thinking and mentality.

My demonstration was met with a mute response from Stella. I think she completely missed the point I was trying to communicate.

The conversation ended with me saying that I had always been grateful for what she did, and I hoped that she felt the same way about what I did. I doubt that my feelings on this issue were ever accepted by Stella. She always seemed to think she did more than me and anyone else.

This was simply not the case.

Stella Hoops & Facts

'Stella hoops' was a name I gave to the feeling that I was being manipulated to undertake a task or do something that Stella thought she wanted me to do. I came to understand that these hoops represented my love and care for her. It involved the need to read her mind, to try to work out what she wanted. Simple household tasks were left half completed by Stella for me to then complete without being asked.

An example would be clothing that had been washed and folded then being left right next to the cupboard where they were stored. Folded towels could stay next to the cupboard for days, if not a week or two, before they were placed in the cupboard. Often Stella would do it, or I would if I noticed, and occasionally one of the children might complete the task. I would simply place the towels in the cupboard without any expectation of thanks or appreciation. This was simply a given with these types of duties. For Stella there was a need to be noticed and constantly appreciated for all that she did around the home. It all seemed unbalanced to me. Grocery shopping, doing the dishes, attending to the dishwasher, and cooking were examples of things which were not completely finished by Stella. This type of thinking did not make living with Stella easy.

Outside and inside the house I simply did the jobs that needed to be done. The lawns were not half mown and the mower left on, the pool half cleaned and equipment and chemicals left outside the pool shed, or the bins half put out. There was nothing attached to the completion of these tasks, no control or power motive, nor the need to feel a sense of gratitude. In other words I did what I did because it had to be done, and I took it as a given that my efforts around the house would be both valued and appreciated by Stella.

Stella required almost constant praise as well as appreciation, well beyond the norm, for everything she did – and not only around our home. It was all about her validation.

* * *

There were times when Stella seemed to lock in and not be able to see another side or point of view, particularly when she was upset or emotional. This type of thinking was impossible to combat. It often involved a complete lack of trust, belief, and the ability to give me the benefit of the doubt.

Stella could think something, usually negative, which would quickly become her truth. If this went unchallenged it could become fact and reality in a very short period. Once the negative thought was cast in concrete it would then be stored in the Vault of Resentment, for later recall and use. If you dared challenge Stella's thoughts it was proof that you were trying to manipulate her, take advantage of her, or look to force her into an outcome that she did not want. This type of thinking was absolutely hopeless to try and deal with.

It produced extremely negative and relationship-damaging consequences.

Love Tanks

Needing to fill up Stella's 'love tanks' was another thing that became an issue once we were married. Of course, you want to fill up your partner's love tanks by doing things for them or saying things to them, without obligation, to make them feel good about themselves and valued by you. The key here is that you do and say things because you want to. It all happens naturally and without too much thought.

A further key here, I believe, is that the people involved are comfortable with who they are, and have a strong self-concept as well as a strong sense of self.

In my relationship with Stella, after every issue or disagreement, I was held responsible to fill up her love tanks. I spoke to Stella on a number of occasions about her holding me responsible for this, and said that I thought it was a rather childish concept. I also said I thought it was her responsibility to keep her own love tanks full. The things that I said and did for her were done both willingly and naturally.

It was mentioned to me that Stella's former partner had said that he, too, had to fill up Stella's love tanks after an issue arose or some sort of argument, disagreement, emotional meltdown or tantrum. This process of having to repair Stella's hurt could take up to a week to work through. You effectively had to be a good boy. It was also mentioned to me that Stella could not speak about her issues in an adult way, and that one had to read her mind to work out what the real issues were.

Perfectionist & Controller

Stella was one of those people who had a perfectionist outlook. In some ways having a perfectionist outlook is an admirable quality but, if taken too far, it can only lead to failure. Whilst admirable to do your very best at everything you do, in order to have balance I believe you need to be able to accept that not everything you do will turn out perfectly. Doing your best is probably what matters the most.

With Stella it was very important that she saw herself as working the hardest or the longest, producing the best outcome possible, doing whatever the task was in the quickest time, and achieving the best outcome possible. Praise, appreciation, and gratitude, beyond the norm, was then expected – and best given if you did not want to have to go through another episode of filling up those love tanks. Criticism of something Stella had done, even if it was constructive, was best kept to yourself. In some ways, it was best to underachieve so that Stella could see herself as the 'winner.'

Another way to keep the peace was to dumb myself down and not do my best but to leave the mantle of success for Stella to claim.

I was also told that Stella's former partner said he lost his sense of self in his relationship with Stella, and once they had separated he was able to rekindle an artistic side he'd had before his relationship with Stella.

I fully understand his thoughts and sentiments.

* * *

It was easier to let Stella have her way, in order to make her happy and to have a peaceful life. Things had to be done in her time, at her pace, and to her level of satisfaction.

I always felt caught between trying to help Stella with a task to be completed and underachieving, so that she could not say I did nothing, while also letting her complete the task and praising her for the outcome so that she felt good about herself.

I was told that Stella's former partner thought his life and time with Stella was all about her, even though *she* thought he behaved as though it was all about him. He simply went along with it, as I did in the end, because he did not want to face yet another negative reaction. Her former partner also said he became submissive to her needs to keep the peace, and that he adopted a 'yes man' mentality.

I can, once again, fully identify with his sentiments.

* * *

Instead of building on the good things we had and working on the not so good, she would constantly be looking at other people's relationships, taking all the good points she saw and wanting to apply them to our relationship.

This was, of course, without being able to see inside the particular relationship she was using as an example. She seemed to only see all the good in other relationships, and glance over the not so good aspects. There seemed to be very little appreciation whatsoever of the good things we had in our relationship, and almost an exaggeration and pursuit of the negative. Once we were married she was rarely happy with anything to do with our relationship. Further, there was nothing I could do or say, or not do or say, that seemed to be able to change this. Happiness, in our relationship, was a moving target.

Stella would also often exclaim in private, 'Why do I have to work so hard? Why do other women have it easier than me? I wish I was famous. I wish I was good at something.'

It was like a Catch-22. In my view, working hard defined Stella's sense of self-worth, but then she felt hard-done by, because she was always working.

Pleading the Fifth

This is a reference to the Fifth Amendment of the Constitution of the United States of America. Making such a plea means that you refuse to answer a question, on the grounds that your answer might incriminate you. However, just because you plead the fifth, it doesn't mean that you cannot be found guilty by some other means.

In the context of our relationship, Stella would think something of me, or that something had been done by me, or form a negative opinion about something I had said or not said. Put simply, if you answered her loaded questions, which could only be answered in one way, you were guilty. Not answering her loaded questions was also a sign of guilt. Anything in between was an attempt to manipulate her.

Letting me know that she thought I was pleading the fifth happened often, in both moments of relative calm and during her vile tirades. In doing this she assumed guilt, a deliberate intention on my behalf to upset, hurt, and take advantage of her, or to manipulating her to achieve an outcome from her that I alone wanted. It was truly ridiculous. It involved Stella having no trust or belief in me as her partner, nor the ability to give me the benefit of the doubt in a wide range of circumstances or issues that a normal relationship faces on a day-to-day basis. She seemed to almost rejoice when, in her mind, she had caught me out. It was more proof that I was seeking to take advantage of her and use her for my own dastardly outcomes and self-serving benefits. It was all very foreign to me.

The end result of all of this was more examples, in Stella's mind, of the manipulative and terrible husband she eventually came to see me as. All this was stored by Stella in the Vault of Resentment, to be used at a later date.

Two things she said were, 'You remind me of my father, you manipulative bastard,' and, 'You're not accountable for being an absent husband who gave his wife fuck-all emotionally, other than lectures on how to be happy within yourself, and you removed every piece of accountability from yourself as to how your actions impacted me.'

Household Duties

Once we had married, the split of household duties was another area of contention that seemed to arise out of nowhere. Prior to our marriage things seemed to be working out fine. In saying this, I acknowledge that the split of household duties is often an area of contention for newly married couples, and can be made extra complicated when children from previous relationships are involved.

To be generous towards Stella's claims that she undertook more than her share of household duties, let's assume that the split between outside and inside duties around the house was 40/60. I did 100% of the outside duties. This included weeding, watering, mowing the lawns, putting the bins out, cleaning and maintaining the swimming pool, cleaning gutters, pumping up car tyres, as well as a constant range of general house maintenance tasks.

Inside the house I felt I more than carried my weight. I was responsible for all the money tasks, including paying the bills, as well as investing and saving for our retirement. I did my own washing, as well as that of my children while they were younger, cooked family meals once or twice a week, almost always went and picked up takeaway food we ordered, stacked and unstacked the dishwasher, undertook the fruit and meat shopping, and nearly always accompanied Stella to the shops to undertake the grocery shopping, so she could not claim that I had not assisted in undertaking this weekly task.

With a cleaner coming into the house on a regular basis, my involvement in cleaning tasks was less than Stella's, but not by as much as Stella led herself to believe. She undertook folding and putting away the clothes, cooked maybe two or three beautiful family meals a week, and ensured that our young children had good quality food in their lunch boxes for school. She almost always cleaned the fish tanks and our pet birds' cage, although these tasks, quite rightfully so, were given to our children to look to complete when they became older. Stella may have also scrubbed the odd bathroom and toilet, if there was a professional cleaning session missed, and picked up a broom to sweep the floors and used a vacuum cleaner on more occasions than I did.

I am very comfortable in saying that I more than held my own with regard to the household duties undertaken within the house. Claiming 50% of the residual 60% for duties inside the house gives me a further 30% to add to the 40% for performing 100% of the outside duties. I am comfortable saying, then, that I was responsible for 70% of the total household duties.

This leaves Stella with the remaining 30%.

Perceptions of Love

I grew up as a child with unconditional love, in a stable and positive family environment. Now, as a parent, having lived a wide range of life experiences, my perceptions of what love is are more mainstream. I fully understand and appreciate the opportunity I had of growing up with great parents. Further, I acknowledge that my upbringing gave me a good sense of self.

I acknowledge that while love is difficult to define, I think my definition of love would follow the way a psychologist may define it along the following lines:

1. *Passion* underlies physical desire, sexual behaviour, and arousal. This is the physical side.

2. *Intimacy* is the emotional aspect, including closeness, connectedness, and warmth of friendship.

3. *Commitment* is the conscious decision to stick together for the long haul.

I also think you can look at love as giving someone the power to break your heart, but trusting they won't. I loved Stella with everything that I had. That is why I married her and made a lifelong commitment to her.

Stella loved, but her perception of love was very different from mine. Her love seemed to be about power, control, gifts, and gratitude.

I was told that Stella's former partner felt his relationship with her was 'managed', that he felt she treated him like a client and not a partner, that she did not love him for the person he was, and that she did not respect his thoughts on a wide variety of issues and topics. He also said that he fell out of love with Stella a long time before their relationship ended, and possibly did not really love her at any stage.

She was, in fact, impossible to love. With regard to Stella's perceptions of love, I found his thoughts to be very true. I remember Stella saying to me one day that she only loved her former partner 70%. I found that comment to be very strange. To me you either love someone or you don't. I got the feeling I was loved far less than her former partner, as our relationship continued to move towards its inevitable end.

I want to now elaborate further on the concept of Stella's perception of love. Power, control, gifts, and gratitude are things I identify with the corporate world. As a result, it is no coincidence to me that Stella thrived in the corporate world. She worked extremely hard to develop and maintain her professional image. Work was her passion, it defined her, and gave her an enhanced sense of self-worth.

As an employee in a senior role, she had far more power and control than the average worker. Her undoubted hard work and the success she achieved resulted in many gifts and expressions of gratitude on a regular basis. These gifts and expressions of gratitude included substantial bonuses, interstate trips, and overseas travel with no expense spared with regard to where she stayed, and attendance at numerous sporting and artistic events. There was never a dull moment.

Stella's role in turning the fortunes of the company around reached crazy heights. One day she even came home and said that she was embarrassed by being called complimentary names around the company for her culture changing input, and happy, bright and pleasant personality. I somehow doubt Stella's embarrassment lasted too long. In reality, she would have lapped this all up. In her work role everything she wanted was happening for her. She had power, control, was receiving regular gifts, and was being shown plenty of gratitude. Something Stella said to me after our separation that shows how much her achievements in the corporate world meant to her was that she had worked hard all her life and had waited thirty years for her career to reach this level, and she was going to run with it. It is little wonder to me that her family life paled into insignificance when compared to her corporate life, in terms of her self-worth.

Stella seemed to employ the same template of power, control, gifts and gratitude towards all of her personal relationships, including her relationship with the family pets. There were slight tweaks to the template with regard to whether power, control, gifts, or gratitude were at the forefront, but all played a significant part in what she did in all of her personal relationships. For example, Stella had the idea of purchasing a pet bird. She also undertook the majority of the care for the bird, as well as initially training him and encouraging him to speak. He was a brilliant little family pet, and when he suddenly died a couple of years later we were all very upset.

Stella showered attention upon our little bird. He naturally responded to her, and was a very good conversationalist. Many of the words and expressions that Stella taught the bird were about her. I will always remember him often saying his name followed by the words 'is mummy's boy, mum, mum, mum, mummy's boy.' In the end the little bird was more her pet than a family pet. That was the way it was. It was Stella who controlled the bird, and wanted to have power over him.

I had a good little exchange with the bird, by having whistling competitions with him. He was very alert and quick to pick up on new sounds and would mimic what I did almost immediately. As silly as it sounds, I felt Stella was jealous of my little time of fun with our family pet.

I remember one of her children calling out to the bird, and Stella calling out as well. Naturally he flew to her. This upset the child, who said, 'He is not a family pet, mum, he is your pet.' We all felt the same way, but I could never understand why it needed to be that way. The bird, through learned behaviours taught by Stella, had a need to mainly respond to her demands if there was a choice between her and another family member.

It is not an easy thing to sit and write about another person's relationship with their children or to be comfortable with offering any observations of your own. We all parent differently and there is probably no wrong way if all is done genuinely in the children's best interests and with the best of intentions. Having said this, here are my observations of Stella's relationship with her children, who, like mine, were living in a shared parenting situation.

I will start off by saying that there are plenty of worse mother's than Stella in this world. Having said this, I observed a relationship between Stella and her children that was over the top. She seemed to need to overcompensate in just about all aspects of their relationship. I am not sure why. Was it about Stella trying to give her children the hugs and kisses she said she missed out upon in her childhood? Was she trying to demonstrate her love for her children to both herself and others with exaggerated displays of affection, or trying to make up for not really being about the place for the first couple of years of their lives due to post-natal depression?

Stella also had a need to return to full-time work as soon as possible after the births of her children. Maybe it was all about Stella needing to fill her love tanks, by filling the love tanks of her children. Whatever the reason, she seemed to need to constantly demonstrate her closeness to her children through exaggerated acts of public affection. It all seemed unbalanced to me. Her children seemed to have a learned response to meeting her needs. I am sure that Stella had no idea that this was how her relationship with her children looked to many people, both outside and inside our immediate family.

After our divorce, a number of people gave the same feedback to me about Stella's relationship with her children. Most mentioned a similar theme of Stella's actions towards her children being a bit like a display. Was it an attempt to convince others that she loved her children, or perhaps she was trying to convince herself that she loved her children in the way that most people naturally do? It was as if she were trying to demonstrate that she loved her children more than anyone else in the world loved theirs.

I was told that Stella's former partner felt that decisions regarding their children seemed to be made on a 40/60 basis in Stella's favour, and that he felt their children were spoilt by Stella. When he separated from Stella he tried to make things all about the children, while also trying to keep Stella happy. In order to achieve this he gave in to what Stella wanted, even though he felt that a lot of things he agreed to were not in the children's best interests.

* * *

Stella's children, from my observations, played Stella beautifully. They were acutely aware of the difference between the earnings of their mother and father, as well as the role they played in filling up their mother's love tanks. They knew that things would be good for them, and they would get what they wanted from their mother if she was happy with them. I often observed her children ask for something they wanted three times, and be successful on the third occasion in getting their way. Birthday parties and Christmases were over the top, and the number of presents and associated costs excessive. To be fair, Stella also did the same for my children. I did not agree with it all and thought it was unnecessary but, like her former partner, I went along with it all to keep the peace.

She was always hyper-defensive of any criticism, even if it was meant to be constructive criticism, of her children. To be fair I think most parents find it difficult to accept criticism from another person about their children. If things weren't going their way it was often not their doing. Other external factors were to blame. Stella also often made the point that her children were the youngest, as well as the least academic. I just saw her children as *our* children, and a very important part of our family. Each had their own strengths and weaknesses. Her children had completely different personalities to my children, but were accepted by both myself and my children as loved and valued family members. One of her children, as an example, was a talented and promising sporting person across a number of different sports, unlike any of mine.

I had what I thought was a good, solid, and developing relationship with Stella's children, that was both mindful and respectful of the fact that her former partner was their father. On one occasion I let Stella know that I was not overly appreciative of her being critical of my relationship with her children. She wanted me to be more tactile with them, but I said that I felt that was their father's domain. I was, of course, tactile and comforting towards her children when they hurt themselves, as I was with my own children.

I sometimes wonder if Stella was jealous of my relationship with her children. I thought I had a very balanced and solid relationship with them all, collectively and individually. I particularly enjoyed passing on my knowledge of various sporting techniques to her children, and was very appreciative of them listening to my advice, as well as successfully applying the techniques on the various sporting fields where they excelled.

My children did not respond to Stella in the same way as her children, and this became an issue. Stella often said that she felt my children did not appreciate what she did for them, which simply was not the case. For the record, I know that my children appreciated all that Stella did for them, as I did, but they did not respond to her in the same way as her children, or in a way that Stella thought showed that they cared about her, or that fitted in with her perception of love. Heightened expressions of gratitude and appreciation for Stella were not forthcoming from my children. These responses were required by Stella in order to give her a sense of power and control, as well as to make her feel good about herself.

After our separation my children mentioned to me that they thought the whole household was run around Stella's timetable, what she wanted to do and what needed to happen for her and her children. They all felt there was a bias towards this, and plenty of accommodation made by the rest of us to ensure it all happened to her satisfaction. It was easier that way.

My children's appreciation and affection for Stella was demonstrated by the obvious distress and hurt they all felt, as I did, when Stella decided to leave our family in the dramatic and hurtful way that she did.

The Vault of Resentment

'The Vault of Resentment' was a name I gave to the place where Stella seemed to store up every piece of negative thought about me. It was a place where no good deeds were ever recorded or allowed for a counter action or reduction in the accumulative nature of her resentment.

Once we married she seemed to have no trust or belief in me, and no ability to give me the benefit of the doubt with any of the actions, words, or behaviours that she thought were negative. In Stella's mind it was as if I set about deliberately trying to upset her, be overly critical of her, and that I was simply not to be trusted.

Stella often mentioned how all the important people in her life – her father, mother, and former partner – had let her down. In her mind it was a given that I was going to let her down as well, so she needed to keep distance between us to protect her from being hurt again. This way of thinking became obvious once we married, and it was impossible to live with. I found it bemusing that Stella did not see or recognise that the common denominator with regard to all the people that she thought had let her down so badly in her life was Stella.

The information stored in the Vault of Resentment was blurted out when she had her aggressive and nasty tantrums. Even these did not clear out the resentment. It was simply stored away again, to be called upon at a later date.

Here are a number of resentments dragged up from the Vault of Resentment that Stella would scream at me during her tantrums:

'You didn't even carry me into the room on our wedding night.'

'You didn't even give me a hug on our first Christmas together.'

'You loved me with malice.'

'You loved me with neglect.'

'You need to see a psychologist and ask them why you deliberately and intentionally did not look after any of my needs throughout the entire relationship.'

These are just some of a number of things that I will always remember her screaming at me in her verbal tantrums in such an awful and aggressive tone. The fact that I didn't carry her into the room on our wedding night led me to ask many questions. How could an adult carry such a grudge for the entirety of a marriage? Did she really believe that, on our wedding night, I would have deliberately and intentionally wanted to hurt her?

It was crazy stuff. None of her resentments made any sense to me whatsoever, nor was any of it true from my perspective.

I was told that Stella's former partner had much the same experience with her as I did in this regard. He said he often could not understand Stella's way of thinking. Stella's former partner believed her outbursts happened on a weekly basis, and were the result of Stella having significant mental issues.

He also thought that these regular tirades were about much deeper issues and that she didn't understand herself. It was his view that Stella was a copy of her mother in this regard. He believed that Stella could not speak about her issues in an adult way, and so it was necessary to try and read her mind to try and work out what her real issues were. He also said that once the tirade was over you then had to refill her love tanks.

We both lived the same experience with Stella, and came to the conclusion that her actions and behaviours in this regard were both hopeless and impossible to deal with.

The Sins of the Mother

It was pointed out to me that Stella was a copy of her mother, with regard to having regular tantrums. The difference with Stella was that she seemed aware who these tantrums were being directed at, and where they happened. They were primarily directed at me, in private, with no witnesses around. Does this mean that Stella was aware of her actions and behaviours, even if she had little idea of the unfiltered, hurtful and awful things that she said and did when they happened? I think so. Her mother's tantrums, on the other hand, could be far more public.

I had respect for Stella's mother, but I have to say that she was a difficult person to spend time around, being somewhat socially awkward and very intense. Time around her was very conditional and managed. By this I mean that Stella would want the time spent with her mother to be limited to an hour or two. In this way, the opportunity for the two of them to clash was limited. When Stella and her mother were in the same room it was always a tense time.

One night we headed down to Stella's mother's for a meal. Stella and I were present, along with one of her brothers, their mother, and two relatives from their country of origin. The usual beautiful meal was prepared and was being enjoyed by all. Stella's mother's meals were always of a high quality and prepared with a great deal of care and effort.

As the meal was being eaten and enjoyed, conversation around the table broke out in the native tongue between Stella, Stella's brother, and the two relatives from their native country. This was a little awkward for me, as I couldn't fully understand what was being said. I looked over at Stella's mother as this was going on, and thinking that she looked like she was about to explode. Her facial expression was strained and her eyes looked glazed over. Although I sensed that something was about to happen, I was still somewhat taken aback when it did.

All of a sudden, Stella's mother stood up at her end of the dining table, banged the table, and screamed out, 'You can all go and get fucked.' Needless to say, the conversation stopped as she stormed out of the dining room. There was an awkward silence for a moment or two, as everyone digested what had just happened, and possibly wondered what was going to happen next.

I left the room and spoke with Stella's mother and tried to calm her down.

When we left a short time later, Stella's mother's mood had not changed and, in front of all present, when Stella said goodbye, her mother replied in English, 'You can just piss off.' At this stage, I interjected and told Stella's mother that what she had said to Stella was unacceptable, and we left.

It is understandable that Stella was extremely upset by this particular interaction with her mother. I certainly had to deal with the fallout. I am unsure as to why it happened. Did Stella say something in her native tongue that offended her mother? Was it to do with issues from her past? Did she feel that she wasn't part of the conversation, or not receiving enough praise and gratitude for the lovely meal she had prepared for us all? I have no idea. The one thing I can say for certainty about this incident is that when Stella's mother exploded at the dining table she looked to me, judging by her eyes and facial expression, that she was not at all in the moment. No apology or explanation was forthcoming. It was accepted, and almost expected, that this type of outburst was just what Stella's mother did from time to time.

Three things came out of this unfortunate incident.

The first understanding was that, for Stella, this was part of the cycle that she had gone through her entire life with her mother. There was a period of good times, although with an undercurrent to the relationship that was strained. After this, either mother or daughter would feel let down by the other, as a result of something that had been said or done, or not said or done, at which point communication would cease or become very curt. The tension would then build up to the point where a tantrum would take place. After a period of no communication, they would resume contact, and the cycle would then repeat, with few lessons learnt by either.

The second understanding was that there was a strong component of 'like mother, like daughter.' There were no apologies after an outburst by Stella or her mother. It was as if the incident hadn't happened, and it seemed as though there was no awareness of the vile and hurtful things that had been said or done.

The third understanding was that Stella was extremely hurt and deeply affected by her mother's behaviour. Her mother's outbursts quite rightly set Stella back, and made her relationship with her mother extremely difficult. She was unable to be respectful or to carry the normal feelings of love between a mother and daughter. Their relationship was an ongoing battle that was extremely strained and somewhat acted out.

The thing that really came to the fore for me out of all of this, though, was how Stella could see how inappropriate her mother's behaviour was towards her when she had her tirades. She felt the pain and distress of them being directed towards her, but could not see that she was doing exactly the same thing to me. The only difference between Stella's tantrums and her mother's was that her mother's tantrums could be in public as well as behind closed doors, whereas Stella's only ever occurred in private.

Seeking Shelter From the Storm

Describing Stella's tantrums, emotional meltdowns, and vile tirades is not going to be easy. I initially want to talk about these happenings in general terms, before elaborating on what was a turning point for me.

The reality was that I had never experienced anything like this type of behaviour in any other relationship. It was all very foreign to me. Sure, we can all get a little annoyed from time to time but, as adults, we should be able to sort through differences for the benefit of all concerned. I always remembered someone saying to me that if you are really angry with someone or something then the problem more than likely lies with you. This is all very true with regard to what I am about to describe.

I was subjected to twenty or more of these types of scenarios over the course of our marriage, but not before. The rest of the time was spent trying to prevent a tantrum, emotional meltdown, or vile tirade. When things were becoming particularly tense with Stella, I even remember taking myself to the toilet and sitting there, even though I did not need to use the facilities. This was done in an attempt to defuse the situation and prevent the tension I felt rising in Stella for no apparent reason.

Prevention methods could also involve removing myself from an increasingly tense interaction with Stella by attending to some gardening, cleaning the swimming pool, or going to the shops – even if these things didn't need to be done.

All these incidents happened in private, which indicated to me that Stella was aware of her actions and behaviours, even though she knew how damaging this type of behaviour was to our relationship.

After our marriage ended, Stella expressed the view that she thought it was 'absolute rubbish' that she had yelled and screamed at me on a substantial number of occasions. She did admit that she did this about half a dozen times, due to her complete frustration with me. Her other comment with regard to this issue was, 'So what!' I can understand Stella thinking this, as after each incident it was as though nothing had happened. There were no apologies, nothing was resolved, nothing was learnt, and then the process of having to fill up her love tanks began again.

I was told that her former partner was yelled at once or twice a week, and that his views on her tantrums were exactly the same as mine.

Stella's full-blown tantrums should have put a normal relationship on notice. It was surely a signal that there were issues that needed to be sorted out. If her outbursts had happened before the marriage I would simply have left. No-one should have to put up with these types of actions and behaviours. After a second round of these tantrums it probably should have been the end of the relationship. To this day I do not know why I put up with it. I admit that I did not know what I was dealing with. I valued our family, and didn't want my second marriage to fail. I kept thinking that I could fix everything, and help Stella to deal with her issues, so that I could get the beautiful person I thought I had married back into my life. A further defence I attributed to Stella to justify her awful actions and behaviours was that she was going through menopause at the time.

So, what was it like to be on the receiving end of one of these outbursts? I cannot actually remember the first one, but think it happened not long after we married. It all seemed to build up over time, and then all of sudden Stella would simply explode. A typical example would follow this pattern: I would be sitting on the couch watching some sport on the TV, and Stella might be in the kitchen washing a pot or doing the dishes in order to prepare the area to do some cooking.

We would, of course, be on our own. I would hear the banging of a dish or two, and then she would come over to the couch and it would all start to unfold from there. It seemed as though these things were tied up in her scorecard mentality, and that she didn't feel enough gratitude for the things she felt she was doing around the house. In her mind, with me sitting on the couch, relaxing and enjoying myself, after well and truly pulling my weight around our home, I was manipulating and taking advantage of her.

Initially, I used to raise my voice back when Stella shouted, and tried to defend myself against the ridiculous things she would accuse me of that were expressed in such an appalling way. In the end I decided to simply sit there and let her vent. I decided on this course of action because I knew what was happening was not even remotely rational. It was as if Stella simply lost herself, and was not in the moment.

I remember looking at Stella one day as one of these unfortunate occasions unfolded. Her eyes seem to glaze over and become sort of closed. I used to think they were like pig eyes. Her facial features became very hard. No-one seemed to be home, and she spoke in an aggressive and awful tone. I was left with no doubt whatsoever that I was her enemy, not to be trusted or compromised with in any way.

These tantrums and emotional meltdowns would involve Stella screaming at me about all manner of things. Issues would include the immediate trigger point, quickly expanding into the amount of work I did and the effort I put into that work, how much money I earned compared to her, the way I walked, the way I ate food, the food I ate, the way I drank, how much I drank, my level of physical fitness or lack thereof, my apparently incredibly loud and disruptive snoring, my dress sense, my hair and haircut, the way I hugged her or the way I didn't hug her enough, criticism of my family, my parenting style, my children and my ex-wife.

All were fair game when Stella was in this unhinged and irrational state of mind, and it was extremely destructive, especially when Stella screamed out her unfiltered thoughts with regard to the normally taboo subjects of my family, children, my parenting style and my ex-wife. She would work herself up into such a rage, often moving around, but always close to my vicinity, screaming at me as well as crying. These occasions would last from three to five minutes, and end with her storming upstairs or driving off in her car. There was no point trying to talk to her. The reality was that she was unapproachable. There was simply nothing I could say or do to make any difference. As I learned, anything I did say or do was held against me and stored in the Vault of Resentment.

With the passing of time and the number of tantrums these occasions became somewhat normalised. Normalising them was one way to cope, the other method being constantly on the lookout for the next build up, doing my best to avoid them by trying to read Stella, and providing her with what I thought she wanted. I also found excuses to move away from her. I often thought about covertly recording or filming one of these incidents to play back to her when she was more lucid. I wish I had managed to do this.

Surely that would have made her see how damaging, destructive, unpleasant, and inappropriate her actions and behaviours were, and make her see the need to get professional help for her own wellbeing?

Days of Dysfunction

None of what I have written is an attempt at character assassination, although I have to admit, upon reflection, that it reads poorly. Stella's actions, behaviours, and thoughts were absolute madness to live with on a daily basis.

Once married, I had no idea of what I was dealing with, but when our marriage ended, it was easy for me to see that it was likely that Stella suffered from Narcissistic Personality Disorder (NPD).

My life issues were simply not relevant to Stella. Support towards me, once we were married, was minimal. I never knew where she was coming from, nor what was real. I could not read her, beyond knowing that she had two modes, both of which were all about her.

The first was Stella in work mode, where there was a conditional environment, power, and control, as a result of her senior employment position, a substantial and warranted wage, gifts in the form of travel, bonuses and corporate entertainment, and gratitude constantly being expressed by all involved for her great achievements and hard work.

Stella's second mode was non-work mode. In this mode it was as if Stella required the people that were significant to her to selflessly be there when required by Stella, in order to fill up her love tanks.

I was told that Stella's former partner felt that he could understand most people, but he could not understand Stella's way of thinking, or recognise where she was coming from. Everything was all about her. I can easily identify with the way he felt. It was crazy and maddening to live with.

Coming home from work for Stella appeared to be some sort of a letdown. Instead of returning to an environment where she should have felt buoyed, loved, safe, appreciated, and able to be her true self, it appeared to be a deflating experience for her. Often, I actually saw this deflation take place as she walked through the garage door into the living area.

It was as though the actions and behaviours that she was directing at me were the same things that she was accusing me of doing to her. In Stella's eyes, I was making her unhappy and she was not responsible for her behaviour, nor did she see herself as having to be responsible for her personal happiness. This responsibility was effectively exported onto external achievements, in both the corporate world and her private life. Out of all of this, she seemed to elevate her sense of self-worth. Stella had to see herself as endlessly working the hardest, the longest, doing the best, and producing the most outstanding results possible, under all circumstances, in order to attempt to feel good about herself. It was exhausting to watch and to live with.

So where did all of this leave me? What was it like for me living with Stella with all of that I have just described?

I came to accept that there was nothing that I could do or say that would make her happy. I lived as though I was walking on eggshells. I was constantly trying to read what she was thinking and attempting to give her what I thought she wanted. My relationship felt as though it was managed. At times I felt like her client, not her partner. I had to work with what I thought were the real underlying issues in order to try and survive and keep the peace, and to prove myself to her. I didn't feel loved, and, despite her claiming I did not listen to her, the reality was she did not listen to me. My existence was all about her. She had an entrenched falseness about herself as well as being pretentious, egotistical, selfish, and having a self-image that needed to be fed and satisfied on a moment-by-moment basis. In the end I simply could not be myself.

Three weeks after we married, all sorts of issues seemed to be popping up that I had never been aware of beforehand. I was somewhat bemused and bewildered by what was going on and so I found myself down at a park near our house on the telephone to one of her friends. I knew this was a most unusual thing to do but, nevertheless, it was a good indication of my level of concern at what was going on. I didn't feel the person I had called was all that surprised that I had contacted them and, to their credit, let me talk about the issues I was having. The conversation lasted about fifteen minutes, and culminated with the person telling me that they had heard all of this before from Stella's former partner. I hung up and walked back towards the house, wondering what I had got myself into. It was too late, I had made a commitment and I was going to do the best I could, and see if I could make things work. I had little idea at that stage as to what was happening, and absolutely no idea what to do about it.

The conversation I had with Stella's friend was the first of many I was to have with them. I did not put them in the best of positions by talking with them about my issues. However, I spoke to them with the very best of intentions and with the desire to try and make things work between Stella and me.

A number of incidents took place in our marriage that, in isolation, are quite possibly normal for a great many relationships. Looking back, I now think Stella was programmed to set about creating the same dysfunctional dynamic in our marriage that she saw and grew up with in regard to her parents' marriage.

She did a perfect job of replicating the destructive dynamics.

Yet More Issues

The issue of Stella suddenly questioning why my car was parked in the garage every night, rather than hers, seemed to come out of the blue. It was as if it suddenly became a matter of status, or something of high importance that this was rectified. The reality is that I moved into the house first, and got used to parking my car in the garage. Apart from my car being newer and much more expensive than Stella's, I was also often home earlier than Stella, and parking my car in the garage seemed like a reasonable thing to do.

I conceded to Stella on this matter once the issue was raised, with little thought or concern. What I thought was a trivial issue was, in hindsight, the beginning of what I came to see as a power play. The outcome of these power plays were nowhere near as important to me as they appeared to be to Stella and, in reality, I just wanted to keep the peace.

This incident was just a taste of things to come.

* * *

The apparent issue of my horrendous snoring came right to the forefront once we had married. It was never an issue during our courtship.

Once married, my snoring suddenly developed to the point where I was soon out of the marital bedroom and subsequently spent a good three to four years sleeping on a single mattress, well away from Stella. Needless to say, this played its part in ruining the intimacy of our relationship. I think that once out of the bed you are on the way out of the relationship, if not halfway out of the house.

I was told that Stella's former partner said the same thing happened to him in the last four or so years of their relationship. It's interesting that we both suffered this fate, and even more interesting that subsequent partners have not found my snoring to be an issue. I was also told that Stella's former partner was of the opinion that Stella overstated the issues with his snoring. He recorded himself one night and his snoring was hardly a problem at all. In the end, her former partner and I both came to see the problem as manufactured.

Stella tried earplugs, and I tried losing weight, as well as a whole range of breathing paraphernalia, but to no effect. I am in no way making light of the problem of snoring. Not only is it potentially life threatening to the person who snores, but it can also be a relationship-ending issue for a partner who is unable to tolerate or adjust to the problem.

I sometimes wondered if Stella had seen her mother remove her father from their bedroom for snoring. Was this just learned behaviour from her childhood?

Or was it a power and control thing?

Telephone Tennis

In Stella's mind, once we were married I immediately stopped demonstrating to her that I loved and cared about her. Nothing could be further from the truth.

One of the things that demonstrated this 'Stella Fact' was that I stopped calling her at work. This was not the case.

Once she had raised this with me, calling her at work became something that I did almost on a timetable-like basis. Sometimes I called spontaneously, which is the way it should be, but mainly it was done once she made it clear that she wanted the calls.

The majority of the time Stella was either not in her office, didn't answer, was too busy to take the call, was in a meeting or about to go to a meeting, or was on another call. Even when I was able to speak to her, my call was often abruptly terminated and she seemed to gain great pleasure out of letting me know just how busy she was. It became a game.

A number of other people mentioned that they had experienced exactly the same thing when they tried to contact her at work, and had made the decision to not bother calling her when she was in the office. I continued to ring her on a daily basis, often twice a day, but came to accept that it was a power game that Stella liked to play. It made her feel important. In reality, it was all about filling up her love tanks. She rarely rang me at work, and when she did, I was often busy with clients.

There were some that were good natured, spontaneous, and fun phone calls. For the most part, however, after we married, the calls I made were designed to keep the peace and try to make her happy.

Unfortunately, they quickly became an obligation.

Darkness & The Light

Another issue that was not a problem prior to our marriage was that I wanted to make sure the house was secure at night by checking that the downstairs exterior doors and windows were locked.

Making sure our house was secure at night was just plain common sense to me. Checking that the doors and ground floor windows were locked was just a matter of being cautious and sensible. Although we lived in a good area, there was always the chance that a break-in could occur, and we often had multiple children in the house at any one time. It made perfect sense to me that to prevent a break-in the house needed to be secure. Stella mentioned to me on a number of occasions that she hardly ever locked the front door of her previous house at night, and that nothing bad had ever happened to her.

In order not to annoy Stella, I undertook the task of locking up fairly quickly and quietly, and often when she had gone upstairs to prepare for bed.

* * *

Turning off the lights when I left a room, and switching off the mains power for small appliances after I had used them also became an issue. I can understand that this type of thing is common in most marriages, however, the extent to which these disagreements became an issue caught me by surprise.

Although I am not obsessive about these things, it made perfectly good sense to me to turn off lights and appliances. Stella portrayed herself as being environmentally conscious, and actively undertook recycling activities with our weekly garbage.

In line with this type of environmental outlook, apart from the cost saving of the extra energy usage, it made good sense to me to try and use less energy wherever possible. I thought it was just common sense and good discipline.

Turning off small appliances at the power point made good sense to me, in case there was a power surge or some sort of malfunction and the appliance caught fire. This had happened to me once in a previous home.

This was an annoyance to Stella, so I let the matter go and only checked on these types of things when Stella was not at home.

An Ensuite of Problems

Stella's children walking into our ensuite area unannounced was also something that I thought had been sorted early in our relationship, but it came to the fore again after we married.

I expressed the view that I thought it was a little unnecessary. I saw our bedroom and ensuite as an adult area, exclusive to us, and not one where children should feel they had the right to enter unannounced. It was not as if her children were not welcome in these areas, if the need arose, but more that I felt it was not necessary for them to be there unannounced. My children certainly rarely entered our bedroom or ensuite area, and only did so if they had knocked or asked if they could come in.

I was also not in favour of her children entering our ensuite area to shower with their mother or sit and talk with her in the mornings as she showered. I wanted this area to be for our own private use without being concerned about visitors suddenly entering our space for no good reason. This caused issues between us in terms of having a united stance in front of our children, and the associated respect for authority.

Stella simply thought I was being too conservative. She took no notice of what I said, nor did she respect my views on the matter and continued to allow her children into our bedroom and ensuite whenever they so desired. Some of the subsequent rather cocky and disrespectful looks I received from them as they did this were difficult to take. Stella was oblivious to it all.

To keep the peace, I once again expressed my view, conceded, and went along with it all as best I could.

* * *

Two or three weeks after our wedding, I felt that something had changed. Stella seemed like a different person to the one I had courted and lived with before we married.

This feeling was given some validity by a little note I came across just two or three weeks after our wedding. To this day I do not know why I did not front up to Stella to seek an explanation.

I was in our ensuite using the facilities, and started to rummage around in a group of magazines that were kept there for light entertainment. I noticed a small notebook which I had not seen before, and innocently flicked through a few pages. As I did this, I came across a note that Stella had written. My first thought was to put the notebook down, as what was written there was obviously personal. The note, however, was very short and therefore quickly read before I had the chance to decide not to read it. The note said something along the lines of me being a male chauvinist, overweight, and that I was going to become lazy and take full advantage of her.

I now believe that this note was deliberately left by Stella for me to read. I was absolutely staggered by what I had read. The comments seemed completely uncalled for.

The games of cat and mouse had begun.

Early Misgivings

Early in our marriage I had some real concerns about what was happening. The person I had courted and fallen in love with did not appear to be the person I had married. From my viewpoint absolutely nothing had changed, but Stella later told me that she knew the marriage would not work out within one week of the ceremony.

She told me after our separation that she thought I had effectively 'put my cue in the rack' within this time, as far as romance was concerned. Nothing could have been further from the truth.

It was as if I was entirely responsible for her negative issues, actions and attitudes, towards both me and our marriage. Her trust and belief in me simply seemed to evaporate. It was very surreal and confusing to deal with. Almost overnight, Stella's demeanour towards me became stand-offish and difficult. Her emotional maturity and stability were more than questionable, and her ownership of these issues and responsibility for the part she was playing were practically non-existent. Her corporate image, however, was holding up beautifully. Through social media, she presented a picture of being happy in her marriage as well as being a dedicated mother and stepmother. All seemed perfect to the outside world and to our children, to the extent that my children said they had no idea that there were serious issues between Stella and me until after our marriage had ended. This is perhaps some indication of the level of act and display that Stella was capable of putting on. Even the children who lived with us were fooled.

Around this time we also planned and booked a lengthy overseas trip with all of our children. It was a bucket list thing for Stella to do, and was a wonderful experience for all of us. The trip was to take place a relatively short time after we married, but things deteriorated so quickly that I thought we would not stay together long enough to take the holiday.

* * *

Following our marriage, a myriad of failings that Stella thought I had came to the fore. She said that she thought I was a 'football fanatic', an alpha male, and a racist. My way of parenting was criticised, and my family regularly mentioned in a negative way. One of the biggest issues she had was my failure to hold her hand in public.

The fact is that I was embarrassed to hold another person's hand for no other reason other than I sweat profusely through my hands. Holding hands, therefore, felt awkward for me. I did try to hold her hand from time to time, but on those occasions it often seemed that she didn't want to. My compromise was to offer to lock arms at the elbow, but this option was rarely taken up.

There was always something she wanted changed. It was as if there was nothing I could say or do that would make her happy.

Tantrums & Meltdowns

The first few times Stella had a meltdown I simply did not respond during her lengthy, aggressive, extremely damaging, and awful outbursts. I have already described one episode that occurred when I was watching a football game. But it is what followed this particular tantrum that I want to highlight here.

After several minutes of being abused by Stella I wanted to break the abuse in a quick and simple way. I reached over and lightly placed the fingers from one hand around Stella's neck, and said, 'That's enough, shut the fuck up!' It worked. She stopped her yelling and screaming and seemed a little shocked. I was disappointed with what I had done and apologised.

I then moved away from the couch and sat on the corner of the kitchen bench. I was looking to conclude or defuse the situation. Stella came towards me and started yelling and screaming again. Without warning, she then called me a 'fucking bastard' and punched me with full strength.

I was really shocked by this, and made a conscious decision not to retaliate. Stella's punch got me at the bottom of my neck and caught my windpipe. It actually hurt quite a lot.

She then approached me again in an aggressive fashion saying, 'You want to hit me, don't you, you bastard, because you hit your first wife?'

That was simply not the case, but I could see that she was baiting me. I told her I was leaving, as I did not know what to do and thought that was the best thing under the circumstances. Stella's reply, once again screamed at me, was to accuse me of walking away 'as you usually do' and not facing up to the consequences of my actions and behaviours. Her final comment was to call me a bastard.

These occasions were absolute madness. It was like watching mental illness rise to the surface, do its thing and disappear, until the next time.

Very sad stuff, really.

* * *

On a number of other occasions, I found Stella curled up in a ball or lying on the bed sobbing, with tears streaming down her face. These incidents would often happen out of the blue and were obviously of concern to me. Of course, I would look to comfort her, hold and hug her, and try to get her to talk about why she was crying.

Looking back on these incidents I think now it was about Stella knowing that she had significant emotional and psychological issues. While she was aware of her issues she did not have the will to face up to them and get the sustained professional help required to overcome them. It was like watching a person who didn't really know who they are, who thought they could cover up a lot of deep sadness most of the time, and who did not trust themselves, what they thought or felt, and had no clue as to whether or not they were happy. She made the choice to do nothing about it except to blame someone else, while running, hiding, and wallowing in her issues. She knew that she was not being honest with herself, and it follows that she knew that she was not being honest with those around her. It was all extremely sad to watch and live with.

I am sure we have all heard the expression, 'The eyes are the windows to the soul.' On these occasions, when looking at Stella, I was able to see into her soul. What I saw was a beautiful person, a vulnerable person, a person who at these times was like a terrified little girl. I would ask what happened to her when she was younger and let her know that I wanted to help her get past whatever was worrying her.

Then, before you knew it, the shutters would go back up and the opportunity was lost. Cover up and denial would take over again, and we were back to square one. I would see the opportunity for Stella to take responsibility for her actions and behaviours fade away.

Anxiety Episodes

I have previously mentioned that I suffered with a reasonably severe anxiety disorder. Episodes are usually brought on by a traumatic event. Suffering from severe anxiety, although more and more common these days, is not the most pleasant experience to go through, and is also something that is not to be made light of.

For me, it involves a sort of out-of-body experience, a disconnect between what I am thinking and how my body is feeling. It's most unpleasant. Your mind can get things way out of perspective. Your thoughts, words, and actions, can be exaggerated or understated. Shortness of breath and a tightening feeling in the chest is prevalent. Now I am on top of the issue. I am aware when it's building up, and can largely deal with it by challenging the irrational thoughts and feelings, occasionally medicating and implementing some excellent breathing techniques.

Without doubt Stella suffered from relatively severe anxiety on an ongoing basis, possibly without really knowing it. Her anxiety was one of the manifestations of her psychological and emotional issues. After we had separated, a number of people in Stella's life said they could see this.

Nothing seemed to be learned from Stella's anxiety, nor did she seem to want to explore or question why it was happening. It was obvious that there were underlying issues that needed to be acknowledged and sorted out. Unfortunately, this never happened. Maybe these incidents were also attention seeking exercises, or some type of warped test, to see how I would react and whether I loved her.

On the surface all appeared well with Stella, but underneath the facade was a very unhappy person. At times I felt she thought I was fully responsible for her unhappiness. It was ridiculous. These types of feelings had been going on all her life, in particular from her late childhood and early teens. Was it all to do with a poor sense of self-worth? Maybe it was. According to the most recent research findings about NPD, maybe it wasn't.

* * *

One afternoon, I was working upstairs when all of a sudden Stella came out of the main bedroom in a panic. She quickly made her way to the window and desperately opened it to get some air. She stood there gasping for breath, touching her chest, and almost wheezing as she sought to suck in oxygen.

I was quite concerned and went over to her, put my arms around her, and asked what was happening. I tried my best to calm her and let her know that she was not alone and that things would soon pass. I told her to do the breathing exercise I was given for my anxiety, which she did. Things soon calmed down, but Stella learned nothing.

I think of anxiety as unresolved issues rising to the surface, a physical warning of psychological or emotional issues that need to be resolved. Anxiety has little chance of being resolved or brought under control if there is not a desire to change.

It is an ongoing process – a journey, as opposed to a destination.

* * *

It was very early in the morning and all the children were asleep. I was on my single mattress in the family area, with Stella in the main bedroom with the door shut.

I remember being woken up by Stella, as she came towards me in a distressed state. She was crying and clutching at her chest, and seemingly finding it hard to breathe.

I immediately got out of bed and tried my best to comfort her. I knew that it was highly likely to be an episode of severe anxiety, but could see that the pain and distress were real and debilitating. I told her to go back into the main bedroom and to lie down on the bed. She said that she had quite severe chest pains and pain down her left arm, and I could see that she was sweating abnormally as well as struggling to take deep breaths. I tried to get her to do the breathing exercises I had been shown.

I then decided to ring an ambulance. Not long after the call the ambulance arrived, and we had two paramedics in the main bedroom with all the necessary equipment. After their initial assessment they decided to take Stella to hospital for further tests and observation.

I was somewhat relieved when this decision was made, as Stella was then going to be in the best of hands.

I thought it best not to disturb the children or leave them on their own, so I told Stella that I would stay at home, and go to the hospital early in the morning to see how she was. I did not get much sleep for the rest of the night.

I called the hospital in the morning, having explained to the children what had happened during the night. I then travelled to the hospital to see how Stella was doing, and when I saw her in the cardiac ward I was genuinely relieved that she was much calmer and in a far better frame of mind than when I last saw her. The usual array of tests had been undertaken, with the 'all clear' being given to that point. Further tests were to be run, and I only stayed with Stella for twenty or thirty minutes, before leaving for a function I had made a prior commitment to attend. I felt like I was in the way, and Stella did not seem to mind. We agreed I would pick her up in a couple of hours, when all her tests had been completed and the results determined.

When I returned, Stella had been given the 'all clear', and so I took her back home. She was in good spirits, and told me that she'd had the same tests, and the same results, when she was twenty-nine.

It was no surprise to me that Stella did not have any serious cardiac issues. It had been fairly obvious at the time that she was simply having a severe anxiety episode, but I could not take the risk of it being far more than that, hence the considered decision I made to ring for an ambulance. You do that sort of thing if you love and care about someone.

What was interesting to me about this occasion was that Stella's mother would do much the same sort of thing on an annual basis. She would have a similar anxiety episode to the one Stella experienced, and end up in hospital for tests. Once given the all clear, she would proudly proclaim that the tests showed that she was as strong as an ox.

All of this was very interesting. Stella could see that her mother's episodes were almost certainly just anxiety attacks, but she could not see that her own episodes were the same thing.

Was it all just an attention seeking exercise?

* * *

If you've taken a sleep test over the years, you'll know it to be a little uncomfortable. I managed to get through the process. I have to admit that it is not the most pleasant thing to have anodes attached to your head with wires sticking out all over the place, and to be required to sleep in an uncomfortable position all night. It can be done, however, with a little bit of understanding, balance, and patience.

For Stella, it was an incredibly traumatising experience. We went to the clinic for Stella to be wired up, and she then elected to come home to undertake the test. From the moment Stella was wired up, the discomfort and difficulty she experienced all night began. There was no consoling her. Trying to get her to calm down, to explain that the test was going to help her, to get her to relax, accept the discomfort, and try to sleep, was a complete waste of time. All night she was distressed, up and down, restless, interrupting the process and claiming that the anodes were glued to her head, causing a feeling of pressure and pain. There was next to nothing that I could do.

In the end the results were compromised, and her ongoing issues with insomnia remained unresolved.

* * *

Two more anxiety incidents of note took place in the later years of our marriage.

Stella was working increasingly long hours in a senior management role that involved at least one or more nights of interstate travel. She seemed to thrive on this. Pictures and status updates appeared on her social media on a very regular basis, showing the airline club, the food, the hotel rooms, the views, beds, spas, and so on, with captions explaining how many meetings she was going to be attending. A loyal band of followers would 'Like' what they saw.

With all of this rock-star lifestyle going on, Stella seemed to have little regard and virtually no understanding of how disruptive her need to work was upon our children and family life. There was no regard at all for the pressures involved in my position of employment, and how much I had to manage so that she could do the things she needed to do to give herself a sense of self-worth. It really was all about her. From an outsider's view, Stella's constant and ongoing absence from our household did not look healthy for the longevity of our marriage.

Stella was living the high life and loving it. There was plenty of attention coming her way, with corporate functions and entertainment to attend, as well as praise and gratitude from a wide variety of people for the great job she was doing. She was in her element, coming home with stories of attention she would regularly receive from men at functions, as well as in bars, hotel lobbies and on flights.

She also had an expectation that I would come and pick her up from the airport when she arrived home, which was quite difficult for me to do in the position of employment I had. In the end I asked her to get taxis home, as her interstate travel was happening on a weekly basis.

Needless to say, I was extremely apprehensive when Stella came home from her travels, as it was potentially a time of significant volatility with regard to her demeanour and attitude. It was as if she experienced some sort of a letdown coming out of the corporate world and into family life. Very sad really. The initial minutes when I greeted her, when she was often exhausted, was a time when I had to be on guard, to try and avoid a meltdown.

It was after one of Stella's interstate travels that she self-diagnosed herself with motor neuron disease.

She had been interstate, looking to win a major client that her company had been seeking to obtain for many years and, to her credit, she had been successful in winning the business. That night, she was taken out to a top restaurant to celebrate her success.

Upon returning to her hotel room Stella found herself feeling unwell. I imagine it was her underlying issues of anxiety coming to the surface again. She then went online, typed in her symptoms, and diagnosed herself as having motor neuron disease. She then spent the whole night crying, and in a state of considerable distress.

On the Saturday morning when she arrived home I did my best to greet her in the way she expected, and she then sat down on the couch in the living area, while I took her bags upstairs.

When I came back she began complaining about how sore her neck was. I said I would take her down to the local shopping centre so that she could have it professionally massaged. I was uncomfortable massaging Stella's neck with the level of pressure she wanted.

I went upstairs to get ready and came back down to take Stella to the shopping centre, as agreed. Upon returning I found her crying on the couch, looking at her laptop and in a state of considerable distress. Of course, I was concerned about all of this and asked what the matter was. She pointed to the laptop screen and said that she thought she had motor neuron disease. I tried to calm her down and to get her to come to the shopping centre for a massage. I knew, once again, that it was highly likely to be another case of anxiety coming to the surface with false physical symptoms. I told her that the issue of her possibly having motor neuron disease would be best dealt with by making an appointment with her doctor, and would probably involve many tests to confirm the diagnosis.

With that, Stella came with me and had her massage. The issue of her feeling that she had motor neuron disease evaporated, and she never did make a doctor's appointment to discuss her concerns.

The second incident with Stella diagnosing herself with deep vein thrombosis also happened after her return from yet another extended interstate trip. With a distressed and concerned look on her face, Stella removed her overly tight-fitting leather boots and said that she thought she had deep vein thrombosis. I could clearly see that it was highly likely that this was not the case, and that it was just another bout of anxiety. In a concerned fashion, I asked Stella about her pain levels and said that I had known of a couple of people who had suffered from the issue. I also said that all these people had said that the pain was excruciating. Stella said that her pain wasn't that bad, which I then used as an opportunity to say that we should just monitor the situation closely. I then suggested she relax in a hot bath, which I ran for her, and said I would get her a nice glass of wine and come back for a chat.

The incident then subsided and was never mentioned again.

* * *

As any genuine partner would, I tried to help Stella with her issues of anxiety and discontent.

I tried to speak with her, and wrote her letters to communicate my thoughts about her ongoing levels of anxiety and work/family/life balance, but with little success. To Stella, all our issues were solely about me. I tried to take this on board but had no idea what she was referring to. I was exactly the same person she had supposedly fallen in love with.

Meanwhile, to the outside world, all was good. Stella was successful in her corporate endeavours, and portrayed herself as happy with herself and her home life.

This was far from the case.

Relationship Counselling

One day, out of the blue, Stella announced that she wanted to give our marriage her all, and that she had made an appointment to see a relationship counsellor. I was extremely supportive and relieved. Finally, I thought we were going to get to the bottom of Stella's significant ongoing anxiety issues and inner discontentment. I told her I was very proud of her, and more than willing to be involved in the process. I wanted us to work.

This particular relationship counsellor had been successfully used by someone Stella knew. The counsellor had helped this person define themselves, and they were very successfully able to move forward. I was highly optimistic. If the same process was followed I hoped for the same outcome with my marriage to Stella.

After our marriage ended, I was told by a number of people that Stella seeing a psychologist or relationship counsellor was nothing new. It had all happened before.

Stella had told me that she and her previous partner had seen a relationship counsellor for about three months, with the outcome being that she was prepared to take it all on board and change, but that her partner was not.

After our marriage ended I was told by other people that Stella's time in therapy had been more like three years, rather than the three months she had stated. She had also seen up to three different therapists, some female and some male, with Stella not listening to the consistent message these people told her. The conclusion that Stella came to was that her problems were all her partner's fault. She thought there was nothing of significance wrong with her that needed changing for the better.

My understanding was that Stella would start to be challenged by these counsellors about obvious issues they saw, and she would then seek another professional relationship. It was easier to run away and not face up to her issues and blame others, rather than making the necessary changes for the benefit of all concerned, especially herself.

However, at the time, I was optimistic that Stella would achieve the same outcomes as her friend, with the same counsellor that they had used. I offered to be involved in any way I could, and was very supportive of the process.

I heard next to nothing from Stella about how her sessions went, if they were continuing, or if anything was being achieved. I did not want to push or pry, and was hopeful that Stella would simply talk about it with me when she was ready. This did not happen to any great degree or extent.

Early in the process, however, Stella asked if I would be willing to go and see the relationship counsellor. I assumed it would be as a couple and agreed, but was surprised to hear from Stella that my session was to be on my own. Nevertheless, I agreed to go and arranged an appointment.

At this stage I was very concerned about where our marriage was at, and decided to be very open and honest with the counsellor. After all, this professional had been of great benefit in helping Stella's friend turn their life around.

The session went for about ninety minutes, during which time I was very engaged and talkative, and answered all the questions put to me by the counsellor as openly and honestly as I could. I expressed how much I loved Stella and how important it was to me that my marriage to her was successful, and how important my family was to me. We also talked about my values, beliefs, childhood, and upbringing. This conversation and information was, no doubt, about the counsellor getting to know me more, and on that basis making an assessment of the type of person I was.

At the end of my session I was surprised to be told that I would not need to be seen again. I asked for further clarification and was told that I would not be likely to be seen again on an individual basis, as this session had given them a very good understanding of the type of person I was. I left with the understanding that once some work had been done with Stella it was likely that she would then see us for a few sessions as a couple.

From here, things just fizzled out. Stella was, once again, challenged to look at her values, beliefs, and attitudes towards her work/life balance, and issues to do with her interpretation of her childhood. It all became too hard to face up to, so she did the usual thing and ran away, leaving nothing resolved. No doubt, in her mind, external factors and I were to blame. I heard little or nothing from Stella about what happened in the half a dozen or so sessions she had. I was incredibly disappointed by the outcome.

I am not overly proud of my actions in the following regard, but I suppose I can justify them by saying that I was desperate to find out from Stella whether or not she was still attending sessions and, if so, what was happening and when I was going to be involved again. In reality, the sessions had ceased.

I found a diary of Stella's, which was not concealed, and looked in it for some answers. I acknowledge that I should not have done this, but I was desperate to find out why our relationship was like it was. I wanted to fix it, help her, and move on to a much happier life.

In the diary I found some notes about me that were fairly derogatory, and a diagram that depicted us as being poles apart, with Stella being willing to move towards the centre and compromise and, of course, me being unwilling to do so. This simply was not the case. I was already compromising in so many ways every day, feeling like I had to prove myself to Stella and that I had to do and say things that made her happy. By this stage, everything I did was to try and avoid a negative outcome with Stella, while still trying to maintain a sense of self.

I also found a piece of paper on which Stella had written her beliefs, goals, and values. This was part of the initial work that Stella undertook with her counsellor. I was shocked to read what she had written, and knew that something was very wrong, although I had no idea what I was dealing with and knew that our marriage was highly likely to be in jeopardy. It was obvious that this needed to be faced up to and dealt with once and for all.

I wish I could state Stella's beliefs, goals, and values word for word, but that would not be right. In brief, what she had written was in complete contrast to how she behaved. Her goals talked about the importance of family, being authentic about her happiness, being kind, gentle, curious, ongoing in her self-development, expressing empathy, and being passionate about things such as creativity, achievement, health, and fitness.

Goals included being more involved with her family and me, having an open mind, pursuing her passions, and learning to relax.

On the other side of the piece of paper were Stella's written thoughts about her behaviour towards me. To Stella, I was largely responsible for her feeling these negative thoughts and disconnected feelings.

In reality, her behaviour resulted from her attempts to cover up a deep sense of sadness, feelings of regret, depression and anxiety, and a lack of trust in what she thought and felt. Other thoughts that she expressed on this piece of paper included not having any clue as to whether or not she was happy, and wanting to run, hide, and wallow in all of this. She was unable to forgive herself for her mistakes and move on with both herself and others. Still having feelings for her previous partner was another issue, as was how to trust that it was safe to love again. I was truly shocked when I read all of this. On the other hand it made perfect sense to me. What was written down here was the stark difference between what Stella showed the world and what she showed me once we had married.

I held out hope that what was written down by Stella showed awareness and insight, but that she just lacked the will-power to actively do something about it. I considered this was all about someone who was lost, who didn't really know themselves, and therefore had no sense of self.

After our marriage ended, Stella told me, in her usual aggressive and nasty tone, that I had forced her to see a psychologist for years. This simply wasn't the case. She both went to and ended the sessions at her own discretion, with nothing achieved, as had been the case on a number of occasions in the past. She only saw the counsellor concerned for half a dozen sessions.

This last missed opportunity for Stella to have insight into herself and listen to her inner self spelt the end of us. It was only a matter of time before our marriage failed. Instead of dealing with her issues, with my loving support, commitment, and genuine care, Stella would go back down the tried and true path of simply looking to cover things up and blame me, others, and external factors for the troubled emotional and psychological state she permanently chose to live within. Stella's personal issues were covered up by more deflection, denial, and mirroring than I thought was healthy.

Stella thought I refused to listen to her, that I refused to take her needs on board, that I told her what she needed, that I physically and emotionally rejected her, that I didn't demonstrate that I loved her by showing affection in public, that I didn't hug her when she needed to be hugged, or make her cups of tea on a regular basis. In her eyes I was a real failure. Time and again Stella clearly told me that I failed to listen to her messages or give her what she wanted or needed. All I will say in reply is that I genuinely loved Stella and tried my best to deal with a person who presented herself as a very troubled and damaged person.

I did not understand what I was dealing with, and Stella did not see that it was her responsibility to deal with her issues.

The Poem

Relatively early on in our marriage things were not going all that well, and I had no idea why. I wanted to fix things, and to help her deal with issues from her past that I thought were impeding her wellbeing, our marriage, and our family. I found myself questioning everything, wondering why Stella seemed so unhappy, and how my actions and behaviours, which in reality had not changed, had changed so dramatically in her mind.

One day I received a poem of sorts from Stella that, to this day, I still do not fully understand. I do not want to seem to be making light of it or be seen to be ridiculing someone else's thoughts and feelings. I have considered printing it word for word in the format that it was given to me, but I do not wish to offend Stella. Instead, I'll try and describe it and the context as best I can.

In brief, the poem showed the thoughts of a middle-aged person who was feeling unfulfilled and unsatisfied, or who wanted to give the impression that they felt this way. These issues and needs were expressed in a way that appeared simplistic and childish. Maybe a nine- to twelve-year-old child would have been happy with the way they expressed their thoughts in the poem, even though the issues expressed seemed far more complicated than that of a child.

The poem mentioned hugs, needs, needs not met, needs versus wants and vice versa, needing to love as well as to be loved, her pain, hurt, and hard lessons always being taught because she felt there was a cold distance between us.

My initial reading of this poem confirmed to me that something was clearly not right within our relationship, and that Stella had serious unresolved issues, as I had now suspected for some time. Reading the poem it seemed that once again I was to blame for her unhappiness. Further, Stella felt that she should not have to ask me to get her needs met, as I should automatically know what they were and fulfil them.

I tried to talk to Stella about her poem but she shut things down, as it was very clear to her that she had expressed what she needed to in her poem. I told her that everyone had needs that they want met, and that it was up to each individual to be responsible and accountable for making sure that this happened, in a way that did not intentionally hurt or take from others. A loving partner would do their best to try and meet a partner's needs, if they were clearly expressed, but they could not be held accountable if a partner's needs or wants remained unfulfilled.

The poem confirmed that I was dealing with serious and longstanding psychological and emotional issues, which would require professional help to resolve.

After our breakdown I showed the poem to my psychologist, who simply dismissed it as expressing adult issues in a childlike fashion. Stella's feelings of despair, expressed in her poem, were victim-like, with me to blame for her predicament.

A Change of Employment

Stella's position of employment, both when we met and for the early part of our relationship and marriage, was at a senior level with a mid-sized company. She worked very hard, was rightfully proud of her achievements in the corporate world, but, in my view, had a poor work/life balance. Work defined her. It had all the ingredients that made her feel important and gave her a sense of self-worth.

Interstate travel was occurring on a weekly basis, although I thought some of this travel unnecessary and believed that it should have been delegated. But this was also about Stella feeling powerful, indispensable, and needed.

I spoke to a number of people about Stella's seemingly over-the-top work ethic and poor work/life balance, and they all expressed the view that this was just how she was. It was her way of doing things, and had occurred in every position of employment that she had held.

In the corporate world, all was going well and Stella was on a high.

With little notice, the business that Stella was employed by changed ownership and, as is to be expected, the new owners reviewed all that was taking place and made changes. Stella's area of employment was one of those that was heavily scrutinised, and the value of her work and output was seen by the new owners as being nowhere near as important or significant as the previous owners had considered it to be.

I later heard that when Stella was explaining her work, contribution, vision, and importance to the business that one of the new owners actually swept her work off her desk, and was extremely critical of the outcomes she had achieved compared to the money spent.

This resulted in me coming home to a wife curled up in a ball on the bed, sobbing. It was as though she was in some sort of shock that an employer did not value her contribution to the business or buy into her vision for the future of the company. All of a sudden her over the top efforts at work were not being valued as she thought they should be. With a very high proportion of her sense of self tied up in being valued by her employer, Stella's distress and devastation were real.

I tried to comfort her, and saw this as an opportunity for Stella to resign and spend some time looking after herself and recharging her batteries.

I put the idea of resigning to Stella. She was surprised by my suggestion but in the end came to the conclusion that it would be a good idea. It seemed a logical outcome to me. We could afford Stella having six to twelve months out of the workforce, and all I was interested in was her personal wellbeing. She seemed to be in a fairly rundown state, physically, mentally, and psychologically. I felt really buoyed by Stella's decision to resign. I saw it as an opportunity for us to get our relationship and marriage back on track.

I wrote a letter to her, letting her know how much I loved and valued her. I spoke about how stressful it was to watch her thrashing herself with the effort that she put into her work life, and how difficult it was as her partner to stand by and observe all this, and not do something about it. I also asked her not to think that she would not be contributing to our family with her time away from the workforce, and that she should simply value the time off and look after herself by putting more time into herself.

Stella went ahead with her resignation. Not long after, she saw an advert for a similar employment opportunity, and submitted her curriculum vitae. She was surprised and shocked to receive a letter letting her know that her application had been unsuccessful. It was no surprise to me that this had happened, and that Stella had not even been considered for an interview. I explained to her that her lack of formal qualifications would have been the reason for the rejection. From there things swung into action. Her contacts at high levels all put in a good word for her and, not long after, she was involved in a strenuous interview process with the company in question. Soon the job was Stella's.

Although I was happy for Stella that this had happened, I knew it was not going to be good for our relationship, marriage, and family life. I spoke with her about looking to set up a better work/life balance from day one in her new position of employment, but to no avail. Instead of giving her new employer five out of ten, when they were used to three out of ten, she gave them thirty out of ten, in terms of her time, effort, and contribution to the bottom line, all at the expense of our relationship, marriage, and family life. Once again, these things took a back seat. The work environment took precedence over everything else. The things that were important to me always had to fit around her timetable and not the other way round, as is probably the norm with most people.

Stella's efforts at work were even rewarded with her being called a couple of nicknames within the firm, based on her positive influence on both the bottom line and morale. Even she commented on these nicknames, and thought that they were a little embarrassing. Nothing changed, however. Soon interstate travel was up to three and more nights a week, and international business travel was also taking place. Our relationship, and Stella's relationship with her children, were secondary.

In the relatively small amount of time Stella spent away from work or thinking about work issues, I observed her relationship with her children being overcompensated for in her actions and behaviours.

The In-Laws

By now our marriage was rapidly deteriorating.

The beautiful, energised, and talented woman I thought I had married had simply vanished. My anxiety levels were constantly high around her, even though it may have not been obvious, even to her. I had questioned whether I was responsible for her unhappiness. I knew deep down that this was not likely to be the case but, nevertheless, felt an unceasing pressure to try and please her. It was a losing battle. Nothing I said or did, or didn't say or do, seemed to make her happy. I was living in a permanent state of anxiety, doing my utmost to prevent a conflict or meltdown.

Stella seemed to thrive on conflict in our personal relationship after we married, with an accompanying sense of infallibility and resistance to anything other than her own way of thinking and seeing things.

I was desperate to make things better between us, and started to try and understand why things were the way they were, and to see whether or not they could possibly be changed. I wanted to find answers to why Stella was so unhappy, why she was projecting her unhappiness onto me, and why she was making me feel fully responsible for how she felt.

In order to see if I could get some answers to these questions, I looked closely at her family. Before saying too much more I want to point out that the concept of family is extremely important to me, and I am in no way looking to be at all derogatory towards Stella's family and upbringing. I was taught by my parents that everything begins and ends with family.

Stella's family seemed dysfunctional. Many divorces had happened amongst its members. Even so, during better times, Stella fondly recalled those carefree moments we all have as children, often with accompanying laughter. She appeared to have always been clothed, fed, had a warm bed, and received an education.

Her relationship with her father was virtually non-existent. She seemed to have nothing but disrespect for her father. According to Stella, he had let her down badly.

I tried to get her to see if she could sort out the differences with her father, and even suggested that she take a trip overseas to see him. All to no avail. Stella's disdain for him is probably best summed up by her screaming at me on the telephone after we separated, 'You remind me of my father, you manipulative bastard.' It was a watershed moment to me. I lived with the blame for all the failed relationships in her life. It showed me that, to Stella, I was inevitably going to let her down. This was a certainty in her mind. She was judge, jury, and executioner on this matter.

Stella's mother lived locally. She was a very difficult person to be around for any longer than an hour. Stella's relationship with her mother was extremely strained, managed, and contrived. While Stella and our family caught up with her mother on a regular basis, these times would often be tense. I was always waiting for her mother to have a meltdown, or for Stella and her mother to get involved in a trivial and unnecessary argument. I tried to assist in some change for the better in their relationship but, once again, to no avail.

Some family situations and relationships are, in reality, beyond repair. This is inevitably the case if the people involved are unable to reflect upon themselves and the role they play. It is also reasonable and normal behaviour in these cases to protect yourself from further damage.

Stella, with regard to her relationship with her mother, had effectively put her cue 'back in the rack.' It was game over. There was too much pain in trying to change the relationship, she had been let down time and again, and could not forgive her for things that happened in her childhood. It was a 'love' that seemed to involve power, control, gifts, and gratitude, as well as manipulation.

On the other hand, I am sure there were times when the problems of Stella's childhood were exaggerated in her mind, both at the time and when looking back. Without doubt her interpretation of her childhood has played a significant part in the person she has become.

I tried to get Stella to change her attitude towards her mother. I talked to her about how I felt when I lost one of my parents, and the need to try and make peace with both her parents before they died. If that couldn't be achieved she could make peace with herself towards her parents.

I said that as parents ourselves, we could reflect on our own parenting, and the mistakes we make. I also talked about how, as a general rule, we all try to do the very best that we can for our children, and said that life would not have been easy for Stella's parents.

I also tried to get her mother to come to our place for tea more often, and to help with the gardening. Stella's mother loved gardening. She worked hard, and I made a point of going along with whatever she wanted to do in our garden, within reason. One afternoon, during a break, her mother started to talk about a sibling that she lost in action in World War II, something to that stage that she had not even told her children. It was very moving, and she shed genuine tears.

About the time I had finished the day's gardening with her mother, Stella came home and, instead of being appreciative and thanking us for our good work, an argument started between them over a very trivial matter. I put a stop to their disagreement as soon as I could. It was all so unnecessary on Stella's part.

One final thing I tried to do on this front was to talk to Stella about the good things her mother had passed on to her. These things included her cooking abilities, fashion sense, and work ethic.

This was to no avail. Nothing changed, Stella refused to take the lead in making any real changes, and her relationship with her mother remained insincere, tense, and volatile.

The reality is that your parents are your first educators. What you experience through them gives you the framework and building blocks which are highly influential in forming the person you become in your adult life. As an adult, I think you become more able to work through these influences in a balanced way, and choose to keep the good and jettison the bad.

In Stella's case she had not dealt with the bad experiences and influences of her childhood, and so they continued to shape the person she was in adulthood.

Spoiling for a Fight

I lost count of the number of outings, occasions, gatherings, and events that were spoilt by Stella's behaviour.

I began to notice that Stella's behaviour was modified and controlled if our children, immediate family members, or friends were around, although Stella could still clash with her mother from time to time.

In the end, I had a sense of dread when we were on our own. The occasion might be a simple bush walk or a meal out together, but I was always waiting for Stella to raise something negative about the occasion or, without warning, for her mood to change for the worse.

I also noticed an undertone of dissatisfaction about everything I did or said. It was as though nothing you would do or say could make her happy and content. She would seem to endlessly compare our situation with other couples, either complete strangers or mutual friends, without obviously having any understanding of the true status of the relationship she was observing. It was demeaning. Nothing I did for Stella was appreciated. She was never satisfied.

These problems were heightened if I had organised the occasion for Stella's enjoyment. It seemed that if she saw the event or occasion as being better than a comparable event that she had organised for me, or had not thought of doing herself, that it would inevitably result in a negative mood swing. This was an impossible situation to live with. The qualities and abilities that others had that were better than Stella's were simply not appreciated by her. Instead, she was threatened by them. On a number of occasions she told me that she wished she was good at something or that she was famous. These types of thoughts may cross everyone's mind from time to time, but they had an extra level of intensity for Stella.

* * *

Going for a walk with your partner should be a good occasion, a time to slow down and smell the roses. For me, it was a time away from our children, and a chance to relax a little and enjoy each other's company and conversation. We had many beautiful bush trails to choose to walk along not far from our home, often with an abundance of wildlife to observe.

Unfortunately, most of the walks we went on together were not all that enjoyable. Stella liked to time each walk using her phone, with the time for each kilometre walked being broadcast from the phone, in an American accent. Personal bests had to be set. In Stella's mind I did many things wrong on these walks:

1. I stopped her from walking faster. I was constantly given the message that she had a better level of fitness than me and that I was holding her back. My fitness level was, in fact, ridiculed by Stella, not encouraged.

2. I walked behind her when the paths were narrow. She did not like this but I felt someone had to, and it was best that it was me. I also did this as I had to be careful where I placed my feet, so as not to slip and jar my knee, which had deteriorated from a combination of my age and having played lots of sport when younger.

3. I didn't warm down as she did after the walk, instead choosing to ice my knee, which would often swell as a result of the walks.

On one occasion, as I was walking down an unpaved slope behind Stella, she asked in a fairly unfriendly and derogatory voice that I try and not make so much noise when I walked. I simply thought it best to ignore the comment, being almost twice her weight as well as double her shoe size.

* * *

Grocery shopping was something I did for two reasons. The first is that I thought it was a part of my normal household duties, and the second is that I did not want Stella to be able to claim grocery shopping as solely her role.

So I rarely missed the grocery shopping. Stella, to her credit, always had a list, and away we went. My role was to handle the shopping trolley, which was something I seemed to never be able to get right or do to Stella's satisfaction. I was always either too far ahead or too far behind, and rarely in the right position.

Another one of my many failings, according to Stella, was that I did not show her many signs of public affection. For some reason, when shopping with Stella I liked to give her a little cuddle in the aisle, or a peck on the cheek, which was rarely met with a reciprocated show of affection. Stella would often say, 'Why do you do this when we are shopping?' as if to imply that what I was doing was staged, rather than completely natural.

Needless to say, shopping was not the easiest thing to do with Stella, but I continued to do so throughout the marriage.

* * *

Date Nights were a little foreign to me. To me, showing your love for your partner is something you do on a daily basis, through all the little things. A special night out is simply an extension of the ways in which you show your partner that you love and care for them.

For Stella, date nights were far more than this. These occasions were about herself doing something for me or us, which I appreciated, to show others, through posts on social media, that she cared about and loved me. It was strange.

Nevertheless, I could see that date nights were important to Stella, and something that she let me know she wanted to do, as she had done with previous partners. I must admit these nights were fun when they went well. We ate at nice restaurants, stayed in nice places, dressed up, and spent what I thought was quality time with each other.

I always felt the need to reciprocate with Stella, and plan a surprise night for her. It was important to not plan better nights – or worse nights – than the nights Stella planned. Planning these occasions, therefore, involved a degree of dumbing down.

What follows is a description of one of these nights and how, in many ways, it was spoilt by Stella.

I had arranged the night out involving an overnight stay with a good friend of mine and his wife. The wives had no idea we were double dating or where we were going. We had done quite a few things with this particular couple and always seemed to have a great time. As a result, I was really looking forward to the occasion.

The plan was to take our wives to an upmarket restaurant in the countryside, and stay overnight in some reasonably classy onsite cabins. Both our wives were told to bring an overnight bag and dress above neat casual, but not over the top.

Stella seemed excited about the night, and kept trying to get me to tell her where we were going. I told her nothing, as I did not want to spoil the surprise.

I came home from work, having asked Stella to be ready at a certain time, dressed according to the standards of the night, and with her overnight bag packed and ready to go.

Stella was working from home that day. I found her ready to go, but still working away at the computer. I was on a reasonably strict time schedule because I wanted to get to the cabin before our mutual friends arrived so that our wives would be surprised. The idea was that I would get Stella to answer a knock on the door from my friend's wife. (My friend had concocted a story to have his wife knock on our door at the cabin we were staying in, with a request for some sugar or something of that nature.) All was in place and ready to go according to our little plan.

When I came back from getting myself ready, I found Stella engrossed in a business conversation with an interstate organisation that was contracted to undertake a big job for her company. My time schedule was getting a little tight.

I let the conversation go on for a little time, before gesturing to Stella that we needed to go. I received a frosty reception and let the conversation continue. Unfortunately, with my timetable now being compromised, I asked that Stella continue the call in the car. Stella's reaction to my request was not great, and she was even less enamoured when I suggested that she transfer the call to my mobile, as it had far better reception capabilities than her provider and could also be logged into the car's Bluetooth.

By this time Stella was extremely unhappy with me and my requests. Although she came to the car with her overnight bag, she refused to transfer the call to my mobile and, with her phone temporarily muted, told me in her usual aggressive tone that she was unhappy I had interrupted her business call. The night was off to a very unfortunate start.

We headed off to the countryside, with Stella still engaged in her business conversation. I was feeling a little flat about what had happened. The atmosphere in the car was tense, but I decided to remain upbeat about the possibly of a good outcome for the evening.

Some ten minutes into the trip, as I suspected, Stella's mobile dropped out due to reception issues. I told her to call back on my mobile, which she refused to do, as she felt her instructions to the caller were now clear.

Night was now rapidly falling, and we were driving in a secluded and dark part of the countryside. Stella's attitude and demeanour towards me were appalling. She kept asking me in a very aggressive voice where we were going and why she needed to be dressed up as she was. 'What could possibly be out here that would be any good?' she asked. I was certainly looking forward to getting to our destination.

When we arrived at the town and Stella saw the restaurant we were going to she seemed to calm down a little. The building was old and rustic and had a nice atmosphere. We were greeted by the owners and shown to our cabin, which Stella also seemed to be comfortable with. I made the mistake of thinking that things were looking up. I was happy that I had Stella inside the cabin before our mutual friends arrived, so that both wives would get a good surprise. Without warning, Stella turned and said to me, in the usual tone of voice she used when she was upset, 'You have brought Anna here, haven't you?' Anna was a previous long-term partner. I was absolutely flabbergasted, but was saved by a knock on the door.

I asked Stella to answer the door and, to my great relief, it was our mutual friends. Stella immediately went into great happiness and surprise mode and the night got better from there. Beautiful wines, social drugs, and food were consumed, fun and light-hearted conversations were enjoyed, and much laughter was shared. We spent the night recovering, slept in, and then made our way home in the morning. I cannot remember receiving any thanks for the night from Stella.

With reference to the comment Stella made about Anna, if I had answered no to this question, which was the case, Stella would not have believed me. If I had answered yes, there was no upside. I simply would not be that disrespectful to Stella and take her to a place where I had taken a previous partner.

It is ironic, however, that people told me that Stella had taken me to exactly the same places she had taken previous partners on our Date Nights. I often found with Stella that it was a case of 'do as I say, not as I do' and vice versa. She could flip between these two positions with relative ease to justify her actions, behaviour, and unhinged thoughts.

* * *

This particular incident was one of the most unacceptable that took place during our time together. Whichever way you look at it, the incident shows Stella at her most emotionally unhinged. Her actions on this occasion seemed to me to border on madness. I was deeply shocked by it all. For Stella, it all seemed to quickly pass. There was no acceptance of responsibility on her behalf, and no inclination to take a good long look at herself, get professional help, or offer an apology.

Weekends were a time where I needed places to relax. One such place was a local sporting ground, where I liked to go and sit alone on my chair amongst nature and watch the various sports being played. It was a 'Zen zone' of sorts.

About mid-morning one Saturday I could see Stella becoming more and more agitated, and decided to remove myself from the situation. I told Stella I was going up the road to spend the afternoon watching the sport. I could tell that she was not happy with this, but knew that it was the best thing for me at the time.

She explained that she had things that needed doing, such as cooking for the family and cleaning the house. I interpreted this as Stella saying that I was choosing to go and spend a relaxing time watching sport while she carried the load on the home front. The reality was that Stella liked cooking, it was a relaxing time for her, but the cooking didn't need to be done at that moment. I offered to get takeaway food that night, which all the children enjoyed. The house also didn't need cleaning, as we employed a very good professional cleaner on a regular basis.

What this was all really about was Stella feeling that she was not appreciated for all the good things she did as part of our household. She wasn't at work, the children were not around and, in her eyes, all my attention should have been on her. I should be doing something to fill her love tanks. I knew where all this was heading, as it had happened many times before.

As I walked up to the sports ground, I felt a sense of relief that I had extracted myself from the situation. I got to the ground and settled in to watch the matches. It was a beautiful day. After a while, with the understanding that I felt another scene was brewing with Stella, I decided to call her to ask her to come up and join me. I spoke sensitively to her about the cooking not being necessary, and also the cleaning being something that could wait for the cleaner next week. I explained that it was a lovely day and, to my surprise, she decided to come and join me. I was pretty happy, and looked forward to seeing her and spending some relaxing time together.

Half an hour or so passed and Stella had still not turned up. I was about to call her again when she rang me and explained that as she was passing by the clubhouse she saw a few friends and acquaintances and had decided to have a drink or two with them. I had no issues with Stella doing this. I saw it as a chance for her to relax and enjoy herself. We agreed that she would come down at half time to join me.

Half time passed, and Stella was nowhere to be seen. My mobile rang again and it was Stella and a group of her friends, all in very fine form. Obviously, a number of alcoholic drinks had been consumed by all, and I was later told that Stella had become the life of the party. The group broke into song which, amongst other things, seemed to be inferring that a certain piece of my anatomy was very small. I copped this all on the chin and, once the song stopped, explained to Stella that I was happy where I was and she seemed happy where she was, and that I would see her after the game.

Towards the end of the game I was starting to get that feeling we all dread that I needed to urgently get home and use the facilities. I spoke to Stella and explained the situation and she said that she was happy to stay in the clubhouse and come home with some neighbours. I was happy with that, as I did not want Stella walking home alone in the dark, in an intoxicated state. I then quickly made my way home and attended to my personal issues.

About half an hour passed and there was a knock on the front door. Thinking it was Stella, I opened the door and discovered that her mother had decided to pay us a visit. I explained that Stella was up the road, and then talked with her for another half an hour or so. I was somewhat relieved when she decided to leave, after a rather strained conversation.

By the time her mother left, Stella had still not returned. I was a little concerned, but comforted by the knowledge that she would be walking home with some of our neighbours.

A little while later I noticed that the neighbours had returned home, and thought that Stella must have stayed there for another drink. I was about to go and join them when there was another knock on the door.

Sure enough, it was Stella, in a very bedraggled state, accompanied by an acquaintance from the clubhouse and her young daughter. I was shocked by what I saw at the door and taken aback. Stella was covered in sticks and leaves, there were stains and dirt on her clothing, and she was sobbing. The acquaintance's young daughter was also crying and distressed.

Even now, years afterwards, I still can't believe what happened next. Stella's acquaintance said that I needed to let Stella know that I loved her. I replied, 'What?' Stella then said in a sobbing and childish voice, as she looked at her acquaintance and young daughter, 'See what I mean. He doesn't really love me.'

I was completely taken aback by all of this. It was extremely confusing, distressing, and embarrassing for all concerned. I then thanked Stella's acquaintance and young daughter for bringing Stella home safely, and politely asked them to leave. I explained that Stella would be alright, and not to worry about her, as this sort of thing happened to Stella from time to time.

With the door shut, and still feeling very shocked, I tried my best to comfort Stella. I suggested that she go upstairs and I would run her a bath. I then went to get some water for her, as she was quite intoxicated and distressed. I knew something was very wrong. What I witnessed was a very emotionally unhinged partner.

Once Stella had relaxed in her bath, had calmed down, and was in bed, I tried to talk with her about what had happened. I was quite disturbed by what I had witnessed. Even taking into account menopausal cycles, and these were not overly kind to Stella, this was a very unusual set of circumstances.

Stella's explanation was that she felt I had rejected her all day, which, from my viewpoint, wasn't the case. As a result, she'd had way too many drinks at the clubhouse, her mood changed, and she walked home in the dark on her own. She became distressed, and arriving at our house saw her mother's car in the driveway. In the state she was in, Stella claimed that she didn't recognise her mother's car and thought I was with someone inside our house and having an affair. This resulted in her going down to a local park near our home, curling up in a ball on the ground and sobbing uncontrollably. From there, she was found by her acquaintance, who was travelling home with her husband and children, when they spotted Stella in the headlights of their car as they came to visit one of our neighbours. She was then brought to our door. It was crazy stuff.

Once again, there was no apology from Stella. It all seemed to pass by the next day as though it hadn't even happened. An apology would have been appropriate, but I would gladly have traded that for Stella to actually think about what had happened, take responsibility for her behaviour, and have the insight to realise the need to get some professional help. None of this happened.

Looking back on this particular incident, I have many thoughts and questions. I knew our marriage was in big trouble. I knew Stella had issues that needed to be dealt with, but I had no idea of what I was dealing with. Did Stella really not recognise her mother's car in the driveway that night? Did she really think I was having an affair with someone in our house, or perhaps an affair with her mother? It was all bordering on the insane. Was it all just another attention-seeking exercise?

In the end, I let it all go and moved on, trying my best to keep Stella happy and avoid these types of incidents. I knew our marriage would end if something didn't change.

* * *

From the outside looking in, we were seen as a happily married, fun-loving couple who liked to hold parties on a fairly frequent basis.

Most years we had held a party at home for Stella's birthday. I can remember four or five of these occasions. Each was themed and well organised, and involved a reasonable level of effort by each of us. They were fun nights and good occasions, a chance to gather our friends together and let our hair down. There was plenty of music, drinking, social drug taking, and general fun had by all. I must admit I enjoyed these occasions and did my fair share of organising, working on the night, and cleaning up the next morning.

Stella didn't seem to acknowledge the amount of time and effort that went into organising these occasions. However, she did seem to enjoy herself. These parties were, in fact, all about her, and trying to make her feel happy and special. She was the centre of attention.

* * *

One particular party I would now like to spend a little time elaborating upon was Stella's 50th. By this time our marriage was not in a good place, and I wanted this occasion to be good for Stella. Firstly, there was a family gathering with immediate relations and all the children at a local eatery, then the party, followed by several nights at a wilderness resort we visited in the early days of our relationship. All my efforts appeared to have been in vain, in terms of Stella enjoying her 50th celebrations. After our marriage failed, she claimed I did nothing for her 50th. She claimed she had organised most of it herself. I thought this was both extraordinary and extremely ungrateful. I put plenty of effort into Stella's 50th birthday celebrations, and not much expense was spared.

The family night at the local eatery seemed to go well. Stella seemed happy, she was quite rightfully the centre of attention, and quality gifts were coming her way. She gave the appearance of being happy in all facets of her life, work, family, and marriage. I knew this wasn't the case, or even close to it.

Next we moved on to Stella's 50th birthday celebrations at our house. I had encouraged Stella to have a 50th birthday party, and to also invite a group of mainly female friends from her past. They were all well-to-do types who were either high up in the corporate world or had been successful in establishing and running their own businesses.

The party was organised, and all who attended seemed to have a great time. I was specifically asked by Stella not to make a speech, and had therefore not prepared one. However, I was continuously asked throughout the night to say a few words. Succumbing to the pressure to do so, the music was turned down and I made a reasonable fist of an impromptu speech for Stella. It was interesting to note that, when Stella realised my speech was about to happen, she interjected in a way that was not all that complimentary or appropriate. Someone got her under control fairly quickly by shouting, 'Shut the fuck up, Stella.'

It was an interesting night from my point of view. A number of people who attended the party also had some interesting observations of the night that were conveyed to me after the breakdown of my marriage to Stella. Most of these comments were around the distance that they felt Stella had developed between them compared to previous occasions. It was as though she concentrated on the people who I had encouraged her to re-engage with in her life, and almost ignored our current friends. In hindsight, this behaviour was probably a precursor to the breakdown of our marriage and one of the first steps Stella took to re-establishing an independent life after our marriage.

I remember enjoying the night, and hardly engaging with Stella at all. It felt as though I was being avoided.

The next morning I got up early to clear up a considerable mess before my children arrived. It took quite a bit of time to remove numerous empty bottles, to mop the floors, throw the rubbish out, and wash the dishes.

The next occasion for Stella's extended 50th birthday celebrations was the visit to the high-class wilderness resort where we had stayed at the beginning of our relationship.

I was really looking forward to us having time to relax and reconnect. I tried to encourage Stella to not bring the corporate world with her via her laptop, but to no avail.

I had also arranged for a couple of our mutual friends to turn up for a few nights half way through our stay. They were a couple we had previously had many good occasions with, and we all seemed to enjoy each other's company.

So off we went to the resort. I was going to try and have a good time regardless, but had the feeling that the occasion was not going to be what I wanted it to be. It took a few hours to get to the resort and, after checking in, we were shown our room. As we knew from the previous stay, the room was beautiful, and the view spectacular.

I was excited to be back at the resort again, where we had previously spent good times together. I turned to Stella to find her in tears. I was stunned, and asked myself what could possibly be the issue that had brought Stella to tears?

I immediately gave her a hug and asked her why she was crying and what the problem was. She said that I had not dealt with the issue of my snoring. 'There is only one king-size bed in the bedroom,' she said. I was absolutely stunned by this. To be honest, I had not thought my snoring was that big an issue. Normally, when we went away for a few days, I was given the privilege of being able to share a bed with my wife. I thought this time would be no different.

I immediately swung into action to prevent another scene. I told Stella that I would go to reception and ask for a trundle bed to be sent to our room. I suggested to her that it would not be a problem for me to either sleep in our room's large bathroom behind a closed door or even on the balcony, listening to the sea all night.

Down came the trundle bed. The resort was very accommodating in this regard, but it did feel pretty embarrassing asking for it. I thought the issue had been resolved. Stella then refused to let me sleep in the trundle bed in the bathroom, and decided that she would do that herself. It would have made no difference to me where I slept. Stella had her usual disturbed and erratic sleep on the trundle bed and, after a couple of nights, in the interest of peace and harmony, I insisted that we swap places. From there we went on nice walks, had relaxing massages, Stella had a facial, and we both enjoyed lovely wines and delicious food.

After a couple of days it was time for the surprise visit from our mutual friends. I had the staff at the reception involved, and I was ready to get Stella engaged in other activities while our friends arrived and were checked in. I had also hatched a plan for our friends to come over to our table as waiters with champagne, to surprise Stella. I thought it would happen smoothly, but that was not to be. Stella could not have been more difficult.

We had both enjoyed a very relaxing massage the previous day. In order to remove the possibility of Stella seeing our mutual friends checking in, I had arranged for them to turn up fifteen minutes after Stella had been booked in for a facial. I also had the staff on side, who were to say to me, in front of Stella, that my fishing trip had been delayed.

Stella expressed her displeasure at me having booked her in for a facial, and tried to get it cancelled at the reception area. I warned staff, and told them to tell her that it could only be cancelled at a substantial cost. Stella then reluctantly agreed to go.

Our friends arrived, checked in, and agreed to stay in their room until lunch.

Stella came back from her facial, which she seemed to have enjoyed, and I then said I wouldn't mind getting a little lunch before we headed out on a quad bike tour with another couple.

Stella then insisted that she didn't want any lunch and wanted to have a shower. I told her that we should have a light lunch and that it didn't make any sense to have a shower, as we were likely to get both wet and muddy on the quad bike tour. She then reluctantly agreed to go to the dining room.

A couple of days earlier I had mentioned to Stella that I would like to sit at a specific table that I said had a great view. It also put Stella sitting with her back to reception, which was the direction our friends were coming from. But, once again, I did not have Stella's cooperation.

I finally managed to coax her to sit at the table of four. She then sat on the wrong side, facing reception. I suggested to her that I would like her to sit next to me, so that we could both look at the magnificent view. Stella, once again, reluctantly did this for me. Bringing about the surprise for Stella was proving very taxing.

I had an indication from the staff that our friends were ready and in place to come to the table with a bottle of Moet. The staff came over to take our order and I suggested to Stella that we have a glass of champagne to celebrate her 50th birthday. Stella declined. I then said to the waiter that I would have a glass of champagne and ordered a glass of mineral water for Stella.

It was a huge relief for me when our friends came over to our table, acting as waiters with the bottle of champagne. It took Stella a second or two to realise who they were, before she completely changed from being incredibly difficult to deal with to what I would call acting out being 'Ms Happy Pants.' She went into overdrive on the happiness and surprise front. I sat there for a second or two with my head in my hands before greeting our friends.

From there, the stay went well enough. It was a pivotal time in our relationship for me.

I remember coming back in the car from the stay and asking Stella if she had enjoyed all the things that had happened for her 50th birthday celebrations. I received a rather unappreciative, subdued, and low-key response. I knew that I could not have done any more than I did. My best simply wasn't good enough for Stella. Was the problem that what I did for Stella's 50th birthday celebrations better, in her eyes, than what she did for me?

Probably.

No Loyal Wingman

Once married, I began to quickly feel that my level of love, care, and commitment to Stella was far greater than her love for me. It was a difficult feeling to contend with, as it made no sense at all.

One of these feelings, although untested at the time, was that if something happened to me or one of my children, such as an illness or accident, I would not have her backing, help, or required attention.

Another was to feel that if one or all of my children needed to move from their other house, as was looking likely, that Stella would not approve of this. She made it very clear that this would have a very negative impact on our already struggling relationship.

A further issue that was made clear to me by Stella was that she would be very unhappy if my earnings fell. This did happen during my time with Stella, for a variety of reasons, but I thankfully always managed to earn substantially more than her.

She also seemed to have no appreciation whatsoever of the day-to-day pressures involved in my position of employment. There was always a mixture of market-related issues, individual client issues, government changes, legislative changes, and the fact that I had to 'sing for my supper' on a day-to-day and year-to-year basis, in a competitive sales-based environment. Not everybody can succeed as I have in this commission-based type of environment.

Everything was all about Stella. Even the family timetable ran around her busy work schedule.

* * *

One instance where Stella failed to show me love and support was the funeral of my first parent to pass away. It was a very intense and difficult time leading up to their passing, and a taxing time for me, as I seemed to have to carry most of the responsibility within my immediate family.

Before explaining too much more, I want to state here that grief, and how we react to grief and the passing of a loved one, is very personal. Everyone deals with their grief in a different way, and therefore no way is the right way. This has to be acknowledged and respected.

With regard to this I was stunned by Stella's behaviour on this particular day.

Being the eldest male in the family I rightfully had a main role to play on this occasion. Some of these responsibilities involved viewing and identifying the body, communicating with the funeral company representatives, ensuring my remaining parent was supported, and delivering the eulogy on behalf of my family. On top of this, I had to balance my own feelings of grief. We were a close family and I was very close to my deceased parent. The last few weeks of their life was a very intense experience. To those of us who have lost a parent, it is like losing the only constant in your life. It is a watershed moment, and a very defining moment in your own life. The reality is that your generation is next.

The day got off to a good start. Stella and I went to watch a couple of our children play in a sporting event. We then went home to dress for the funeral.

As we were dressing, Stella announced out of the blue that she would not be coming with me to the funeral but would go in her own car, as she was taking one of her children to a birthday party. I remember being absolutely flabbergasted. Time was tight for me, so I accepted her decision and headed off to get my children from their mother's house.

On the way to pick up my children, Stella's decision played on my mind, and was competing with a whole range of other personal emotions. I simply could not understand why my wife was not with me. If the situation had been reversed, my children would not have even thought of asking to go to a birthday party on such a defining day as a family funeral.

Now, every time I take a certain bend in the road on the way to pick up my children from their mother's house, I remember screaming out at the top of my voice as I looked across at the vacant passenger seat in my car, 'Where the fuck is my wife?'

I arrived at the funeral with my children, and immediately went into 'get this right' mode. I greeted my other parent, family members, and the funeral company staff, before accompanying those who wanted a final viewing. I went over my notes for the eulogy, and sat with my remaining parent, who was understandably distressed.

By this time it was about three minutes or so before the funeral was to commence. People were starting to enter the chapel and, as I turned off my mobile, I noticed that Stella had sent me a text. She was caught in traffic and was on her way with her children, after picking up the child who had been at the birthday party. Literally one minute before the funeral commenced and I was to deliver the eulogy, she entered the chapel with her children and, unbelievably, sat in the row behind me. A nice comforting pat on the back, some comforting words, or a squeeze of the hand would have been nice just before I got up to speak. But that was not to be.

The funeral went well, I was told, but it was all a bit of a blur for me. Before I knew it, we were all out in the lounge area for the traditional light refreshments and condolences. I, of course, supported my family members and remaining parent. It would have been nice to have had the company and support of my wife as well, but she was nowhere to be seen. She had apparently left, in order to take her child back to the birthday party.

The next time I saw her was at the private family wake, where she sat next to me, which was nice. We obviously went back to our house in different cars.

My wife, as I remember, did not once express her sorrow or condolences to me on the loss of my parent.

For weeks afterwards I was very troubled by all of this. It really played on my mind, to the extent that I rang Stella's friend to chat about it. Their words to me were that Stella's behaviour on the day was noticed by quite a few people, who described it as 'bizarre.' They then mentioned some things that Stella's mother had also said on the day that were incredibly inappropriate and, if they weren't seen as inappropriate, they were, in fact, quite funny.

Stella's mother apparently came into a group of people at the funeral and told everyone how sad she was too, because she'd had to put her dog down a couple of days before. Is this an appropriate conversation to have at the funeral of a human being? I think not. I will refrain from commenting any further.

The second thing Stella's mother did was to ask two of our children to go to her car after the funeral, because she had been to a butcher in the hills and had got them both some of their favourite fritz. I will also refrain from commenting any further here as well.

All of this really played on my mind. I should have spoken to Stella earlier about it all, but it was about a month later before I did. We were lying in bed when I finally decided to bring up the topic of my perceptions of her behaviour on the day of the funeral. Stella was somewhat taken back by what I said, and seemed genuinely upset by the fact that I was distressed by what I thought was a lack of support from her.

I think she apologised, but I mainly remember her saying that she did support me by allowing me to go to the hospital nearly every night over many weeks, as well as doing the washing and folding the towels. This explanation left me speechless.

I was left to ponder whether or not Stella and her mother were actually capable of feeling empathy on these types of occasions. I was grateful that they both came to pay their last respects, but I felt that their behaviour was off, and not in the moment, on the day.

I was later told about a conversation that Stella had with a friend, in regard to what I had said to Stella about my perception of her behaviour at the funeral. Stella expressed the view that I was, once again, being critical of her, as well as unreasonable with what I had said. As I understand it, they then told Stella that her behaviour on the day was bizarre, and that there was no satisfactory explanation or excuse. As mentioned previously, we all cope with grief in different ways and over varying time periods.

In closing, this incident really affected me. I would have left Stella there and then, but I wanted to give her the benefit of the doubt. If I had thought for one minute that Stella's apparent lack of empathy towards me on the day of the funeral was intentional, we would have been finished.

I still wonder sometimes if Stella's behaviour at the funeral was a result of her not being the centre of attention, or her thinking ahead about the funerals for her parents that were obviously going to happen. Was it jealously of our family and how close we were to each other? Or simply the result of not being able to feel empathy? I remain mystified.

* * *

This is another occasion where Stella completely missed the point in terms of being able to support me. My good friend had lost his wife to cancer after a long and difficult battle, and I wanted to support him by attending the funeral. I asked Stella to come with me.

'Why would I come, I didn't know her,' she said. 'I cannot get time off of work, anyway, I'm too busy.'

I think she completely missed the point of me asking her to accompany me to the funeral.

* * *

Towards the end of our marriage my surviving parent had an extended period of time in hospital. Severely broken bones were involved, as well as a range of age-related issues.

During this time I was doing my best to look after the interests of my parent, as well as working full-time, managing our family life, and trying to keep a failing marriage from falling apart.

Although I understood that Stella could not do that much to help out, some sort of support, comfort, or an expression of empathy for the situation would have been appreciated. None was forthcoming.

Simple questions such as, 'How are they going?' or, 'Can I do anything to help?' would have been well received.

Instead, Stella went on with her life, completely work-focused, and travelling interstate two or three times a week, oblivious to what I was going through and attempting to juggle. She was not at all in the moment, apart from living in her own head.

Once again, I felt completely alone, and felt that Stella's behaviour was not what you would expect of a loving and committed partner.

However, I stayed in the marriage. This was because I was exhausted, and psychologically and emotionally shot to pieces. I had nothing left. I didn't want another failed marriage, and to put all our children through that awful and damaging process.

To a large degree, I think I had also become conditioned to thinking that it was normal not to expect support from Stella.

* * *

After a couple of GP and plastic surgeon appointments, it was recommended that I have a cancerous growth removed from the side of my face. Although it was only day surgery, it was not going to be the most pleasant experience to go through. It would take about half an hour on the table under local anaesthetic, and require fifteen stiches to be applied to the wound.

I spoke to Stella a couple of times about the surgery, but it was clearly not an issue of concern for her. She went about her business, did not record the date of my day surgery in her mind, and was completely unaware of what was going on for me on the day of the operation. If the situation had been reversed I would have been there for Stella, and this, of course, would have been expected of me.

I left work early to attend the surgery, and was shown far more concern and empathy by my personal assistant than by my wife. Somewhat apprehensive, I arrived at the surgery, and before long I was on the table being operated on. It was not all that enjoyable. A number of small numbing needles were inserted around the cutting area, followed by large needles containing the local anaesthetic.

The cutting out of the cancerous growth took place, with an area of margin, and stiches were applied to the wound before the area was covered with a surgical dressing. I was relieved when it was all over.

I made my way to the reception area, and the nurse was surprised to see that no-one was there to drive me home. I mentioned I was on my own and was then asked to wait a further thirty minutes before I drove, to ensure that I was going to be up to the task. I waited the required time and, although I was feeling sore and the side of my face was fairly swollen, I was given permission to drive home.

On the way Stella rang on my mobile, completely unaware of what I had just been through. She was in one of her bright and jovial moods, and asked what we were going to be doing that night, as it was the start of the weekend. She commented on my slurred speech and I then explained to her that I had just had the day surgery to remove the cancerous growth from the side of my face that I had told her about. I also explained that my face was quite swollen, numb, and sore.

Little sympathy was forthcoming from Stella and, as mentioned previously, she was completely unaware that my surgery was taking place that day. I said that I would meet her at home and would be looking to relax that night and take things easy, as I had been instructed to do.

$$* * *$$

Towards the end of our marriage, I practically forced myself to have a long cry in an attempt to let the tension within my body subside.

This particular night all our children were in the house and asleep. It was early in the morning. I was unable to sleep and full of anxiety. Lying in my bed with the door shut to the main bedroom and Stella, as usual, asleep in that bedroom, I was wondering what it was all about, and whether there was any point continuing with the marriage. I felt as though I was living on the outside of the marriage. True and real closeness and emotional connection simply weren't present.

I didn't want to disturb anyone, but knew I had to release the tension in my body. I went downstairs and somehow managed to force myself to cry for about half an hour. It was a great relief.

During this time, Stella came downstairs for her normal midnight snack and was somewhat surprised to see me in the state I was in. She sat next to me and offered some comfort, which was appreciated. We talked for a short period about what was upsetting me, at a shallow level. She then went to get her snack, I returned to my bed, and she returned to her bed. Nothing was said the next day, or ever again, about what had happened that night.

In all honesty this was just another time where it seemed as if Stella just was not interested in our, or my, issues. It seemed as though, in her view, my issues were my issues. There was next to no empathy, support, or understanding. It was an incredibly lonely feeling.

* * *

Towards the end of our marriage I also felt that Stella made an effort to actually turn all the children against me. In her mind, it was her and the children against me. She tried, for want of a better expression, to recruit the children to her cause, and have the children see many of the issues that *she* had with me as being their issues as well.

This tactic was never going to work for Stella with my children. Our love for each other was unconditional, real, and strong.

Never Good Enough

The joy and reward I get from seeing others improve or help themselves as a result of my input or support is reward enough for me. I don't expect anything back in return.

I can imagine Stella putting up very good arguments that I gave her no support whatsoever during the time we spent together. In reality, this simply wasn't the case.

After our separation, Stella said I needed to see a psychologist and ask them why I deliberately and intentionally did not look after any of her needs throughout the entire relationship.

The reality is that I was very supportive of Stella throughout the courtship phase of our relationship and throughout the marriage. I did my very best to try and make her happy on a day-to-day basis. Many things were done for her, willingly and naturally, that were not appreciated.

There was the difference in household duties that Stella would deny, as well as supporting her in her all-important corporate career, encouraging her to change employment positions when one became too much, and suggesting she see a psychologist for her personal and emotional issues. I tried my best to help her with her almost non-existent relationship with both her parents, as well as her psychological and emotional issues.

I would pick things up for her and look after our children during work hours, as she would be too busy. I frequently attended training and sporting events that her children were participating in, and also managed to continue meeting the requirements of my own employment position where I, in fact, earned well in excess of Stella.

There were also regular parties, gifts, and holidays that I arranged for Stella.

One of the big issues that developed once we married, was Stella's expectation that I would both drop her off and pick her up from the airport for the numerous interstate and international trips she made as part of her employment. It was difficult for me to fit this in, and still meet the requirements of my own employment. I thought it was reasonable to expect her to get to and from the airport using corporate travel vouchers.

My reluctance to provide this level of support was seen as a failure by Stella. Was this about Stella thinking I didn't care about her? Perhaps it was a Stella Hoop that I failed to jump through. Then again, the motivation could have been some sort of need to have power and control over me.

Other people in her office did not seem to have the same expectation of their partners. In the end I did not go to the airport to assist with Stella's frequent travels.

On one occasion that I did pick her up from the airport, I had just attended a massive funeral for a beautiful lady whom I played tennis with for many years. When Stella arrived, she was upset that I didn't greet her with the required amount of enthusiasm, or hold and hug her both long or tightly enough. She was particularly critical of the hug I gave her. I said I was very happy to see her and took her bags as we walked back to the car. I explained that I did not mean to have her feel the way she did, and that I had just been to a massive funeral and was feeling a little flat and upset. None of this seemed to matter. I was in the wrong, yet again.

My greetings at the airport were an ongoing issue for Stella. Of course I was happy to see Stella and have her back home, but it seemed as if she wanted a brass band to meet her. I actually thought of hiring one to do exactly that.

The last time I picked Stella up from the airport was when she was returning from an interstate business trip. She had been away for a couple of days. Things with our marriage were not good, but I rang Stella and asked her if she would like me to pick her up, as it was a Sunday. She seemed happy with my suggestion and that made me feel good about her coming home.

I arrived at the airport early and greeted Stella with a big hug and a kiss as she came into the reception area. I took her bags and held her hand as we walked down to collect her luggage. Still holding her hand, having collected all her luggage, I suggested we have a quick cup of coffee and a chat before we headed home. Stella seemed open to this idea, and everything seemed to be on track.

After our coffee and chat we headed back to the car, still holding hands and with me carrying all of the luggage. At the car I opened the door for Stella, before placing her luggage in the boot.

At this stage I thought I had done everything that Stella expected and wanted from me when I picked her up from the airport. I jumped in the driver's seat, feeling pleased with myself that things between us had got off to a good start. I passed a comment to Stella that I was happy to see her and that I would continue to do what I had just done each time I picked her up from the airport. She replied, saying it was good but that it was 'staged, scripted, and false.'

I was ready to give up. I could never win. I found myself trying to do the impossible, and attempting to read her mind. When I did what I thought she wanted, it was not what she wanted. It was all about her having power and control. That was what her perception of love was all about.

One of the last outings we had as a married couple was to a community event that Stella was largely responsible for organising. It was definitely something that Stella could be proud of.

The night was cold, and it was raining, so I was holding an umbrella over Stella, and I had also put my coat around her so she would not get cold. People were greeting her and she was greeting people with her bubbly and positive personality.

Suddenly, having just greeted someone, she turned to me and, in a quiet voice, directed an extremely derogatory comment towards me. She was not happy with something I had said or done. I had little idea about what I had done. I thought I was doing all I could to support her.

I was really taken aback, and quietly told her that I was tired of her speaking to me in that fashion. I said it was unacceptable, and it would be in her best interests not to do so again.

Things calmed down from there, but enough was enough. I had

better things to do than stand around in the rain and cold and let myself be spoken to and treated in such a disrespectful manner. All I was trying to do was support her.

These interactions with Stella became the norm towards the end of our marriage. I watched as she communicated with her work colleagues, bosses, peers, and our children in a far more appropriate manner than she communicated with me.

The state of our marriage was very poor. Once again, I had no idea with what I was dealing with, or what to do. All I knew was that I wanted things to work between us.

In the very last months of our marriage, Stella developed some unfortunate dental issues. In the end, molar tooth extraction was required as well as a bridge implant.

We were at a local restaurant, when all of a sudden Stella complained of severe tooth pain. After a short time she left the restaurant in a distressed state, and sat in the car. I was very concerned about Stella's level of pain and wanted to get her home as soon as possible to see if we could get her more comfortable.

I got her into bed and dosed up on painkillers in an attempt to ease her pain. She was quite distressed, and had a restless night.

Stella's pain continued for another day or so before she made an appointment with her dentist. The dentist attempted to ease her pain with a drilling process, but when this failed she was referred to a specialist.

I took a day off work in order to get Stella to all of these appointments, as this was the right and expected thing to do. It was finally recommended by the specialist to have her tooth extracted. We were both expecting the extraction to take place there and then, and were disappointed to be told that we had to return to her local dentist for the procedure to be undertaken. Thankfully, her dentist was willing and able to accommodate Stella almost immediately.

By this time she was a little anxious. In order to help with this I was given permission by the dentist, at Stella's request, to sit in the surgery with her while her tooth was extracted under local anaesthetic.

She coped very well with the procedure and, within a short time, her troublesome tooth had been removed. It was easy to see what the problem was, with a large crack running down the side of the tooth and into the root area.

While Stella recovered, the dentist explained that she would need a bridge to be placed in the gap where the tooth had been extracted, in order to stabilise her other teeth. He then placed a bone graft into the gap and we went home.

A couple of months later, once the bone graft had taken, I took another day off work to accompany Stella to her dentist for her dental surgery under full anaesthetic, in order to have the implant placed into the bridge in her mouth.

This procedure took place just before our separation. As we got out of the car, I tried to give her some comfort by holding her hand. Stella made a sort of grunting noise as she pulled her hand back from mine. We then made our way to the dentist's reception area.

I signed all the necessary paperwork to take responsibility for her for the next day or two following the procedure, and Stella was taken into the surgery.

I came back, as requested, about an hour or so later to find a fairly sedated Stella in the recovery area. I was relieved to learn all had gone well.

From there I took her home, put her into bed, and followed the recovery advice she had been given with regard to medications and pain relief.

All went to plan, and Stella was back at work within a couple of days.

I find this particular incident of care and concern quite funny to reflect on when I think about the comments she made to me about 'deliberately and intentionally not looking after any of her needs' during our relationship. Our marriage ended within days of this particular occasion, so Stella's claims that I did not look after any of her needs during our relationship were unfounded.

I cannot recall that my care and concerns were appreciated by Stella, or even that I received a simple 'thank you' for helping her with her significant dental issues.

Pictures That Tell a Thousand Words

Stella created a number of pictures and family-orientated memorabilia that, ties into the themes of acting out and overcompensating. One day she came up to me with two pieces of family memorabilia in her hands. She seemed to be in an unhappy state of mind.

The first piece of memorabilia was a heart-shaped picture frame, containing pictures of Stella and me from the many occasions we had spent together. We both seemed happy in all of the pictures, and I could fondly recall all the occasions.

The second piece of family memorabilia was what is known as a 'life tree.' It comprised a diagram of a tree, onto which many family-orientated words were superimposed. These words included all our names, our parent's names, and words such as joy, love, happiness, and forever.

Both of these pieces of family memorabilia were well-presented and artistic. I complimented Stella on how good they both looked and asked her why she had not hung them on the wall, as she had done with a number of other similar items of memorabilia.

I was stunned when she responded by telling me this was how hard she worked 'to try and feel a part of this family.' I remember expressing the view to Stella that she didn't or shouldn't feel the need to do this type of thing to feel that she was loved. That was a given. I was dumbfounded.

After our separation, I remember our cleaner saying to me that she had cleaned many houses and, from what she saw, she could make a reasonable assessment of the type of family and the family life within the home. She said our house had way too many pieces of family memorabilia hanging on the walls. It was as though someone was trying to convince themselves that they were a loved part of the family, or trying to demonstrate to others that this was the case. She said if someone actually felt the feelings they were trying to portray there would be no need to demonstrate them to others.

Another example of this type of thing is two wedding photos that Stella created. They were both beautifully presented and artistic, but to me they were a little strange. Thankfully they were never framed or put up on the walls of our home.

Stella looked stunning in both photos. She had then embedded a range of words including 'love', 'happy', 'wedding', 'special', 'joy', and 'forever' into the photo outlines. Although they looked very artistic I thought they were a little strange and unnecessary. It was as though Stella was trying to convince herself, and others, that she felt feelings that she should have naturally felt.

The comment Stella made to me after our marriage failed, that I had married a broken person who never really emotionally committed to the marriage, rings out loud and clear now. Stella was faking it, even on our wedding day. She married for reasons other than a genuine love for me and our family. How sad, for all concerned.

The End is Nigh

Around this time our marriage was in its death throws. I had no idea what was happening, and while I knew something was terribly wrong I didn't know what to do about it. I wanted to fix things and still had this silly thought that all would be alright in the end.

My anxiety levels were off the radar again, and I had the good sense to resume taking my medication.

There were many mixed signals. Four or five weeks before our marriage ended, Stella told me that she still loved me. I told Stella that I loved her as well, and hoped things would work out soon. In hindsight I was being naively optimistic in responding to Stella's claim that she still loved me. Within a week or so she was telling me that, while she loved me, she wasn't in love with me anymore. Game playing, for sure.

Some work that Stella requested be undertaken was being done in one of the children's bedrooms, but that made no sense if she was about to end our marriage.

Some of the children were also given new mobile phones and the contract debit taken from our joint bank account. They were twenty-four month contracts, and this also made no sense if Stella was considering leaving our marriage.

On the other hand, Stella was still going interstate two or three nights a week in the last month or our marriage and, each time she came back, she told me that our marriage was over.

I was completely confused and very upset by all of this. In the end I looked forward to her going interstate, and dreaded her coming home. It was a very distressing time for me. I strongly suspected that Stella had started to see someone else, and had put her boots under their bed. A mutual friend came to the same conclusion as a result of looking at Stella's posts on social media.

By this time I was absolutely beside myself. My marriage was disintegrating, but I was desperate to try and make things work. I didn't think I was the issue, but Stella did. In her eyes I was entirely to blame for the state of our marriage. I was even questioning myself.

For years I had felt pressure from Stella to do things for her, including getting her a cup of tea every morning, giving her massages in bed, and having cheese, savoury biscuits, and a glass of wine ready for her when she came home from work.

These are things you do willingly as a sign of love, not something to be expected or demanded on a daily basis. Making me feel pressured to do these things was about Stella's unfortunate perceptions of love and, most definitely, about power and control over me.

Nevertheless, towards the end of our marriage, I started to regularly, as opposed to occasionally, make Stella a cup of tea every morning and delivered it to our ensuite. I gave her massages in bed on demand, and set cheese, biscuits and a glass of wine on the kitchen bench when she came home.

It was no surprise to me that these actions, which were all designed to try and make Stella feel loved, were not appreciated.

She was critical of the way I made her cup of tea. I didn't have it at the right strength. On one occasion she told me off for 'aggressively' placing the cup on the cabinet in the ensuite. This was not the case. I simply slipped on some water. Stella, of course, rejected that explanation. There was no point contesting the matter. If I had tried to explain further then she said I was being manipulative and, if I didn't defend myself, I was guilty of what she thought I had done. I could not win.

The cheese, biscuits and glass of wine were also a failure on my behalf. In the end she simply walked passed them and ignored what I had done for her. It was a hopeless situation and one that could obviously not last.

I had allowed myself to become degradingly subservient. I knew I was doing this. I wanted to see what would happen if I gave Stella everything she had been asking for. Of course, none of this changed a thing. I remember her saying, after our marriage failed, that I did 'come to the party' in the end, but in a very staged manner.

My Final Letter

Our marriage was very close to ending, and my anxiety levels were as high as they had ever been.

In a last-ditch attempt to save our marriage I decided to write a letter to Stella. I was hoping that my letter would be received in the way it was intended, and would result in saving our marriage and family. This was very important to me, and would require professional help. I was hoping that Stella would buy into my letter. I put everything on the table. We either got some professional help or separated.

My letter was as genuine a piece of correspondence as I have written. Apart from describing that I still loved her, telling her how proud I was to have her as my wife, and saying that I wanted things to work out, I described my disappointment at the point our marriage and relationship had reached, explained how difficult it was to live with her issues and work commitments, and assured her that I took on board the things she was saying about me. I also told her that I was going to see a psychologist, as she had requested.

I wrote how I felt that she saw me as her enemy, that I felt unsupported by her, and believed that she took the view that I could not be trusted and believed in, or given the benefit of the doubt. I described how I had not been able to break down her walls, her Vault of Resentment towards me, her conditional and scorecard mentality, her need to have to be constantly validated, and her battle to be happy within herself. I expressed the view that I had tried my very best to help her with her personal unhappiness, that I had never intended to hurt her in any way, and that I was always there for her. I also mentioned that she would have to resolve her personal issues of inner unhappiness with professional help as I had exhausted all my ideas. I expressed the view that the solution to her personal unhappiness lay within her.

I also mentioned a long list of physical ailments she had which I believe were anxiety related.

Importantly, I thought, I expressed the view that this would all take time, and not just a matter of weeks, to work through. I also expressed the view that if I was making her as unhappy as she appeared to be, we should separate.

The summary of this letter may lead you to think it was very negative and damning of Stella. This was not the case, and a couple of people I showed my letter to after the end of our marriage agreed.

My psychologist told me that the letter was beautifully written. 'It comes from the heart,' the psychologist said. 'There is no blame, accusation, or criticism of Stella whatsoever. You simply described where things were for you, you present a sensible and adult way forward, and a willingness to be a part of that way forward.'

Needless to say, my letter was extremely poorly received by Stella, and it probably marked the end of our marriage.

It was as though I had walked along a beach, picked up a rock, and exposed a sand crab. The crab, fully exposed, then scuttled off to find another safe haven under another rock. In my view, the letter to Stella served as a signal for her to move on, yet again. In hindsight, my letter to Stella represented nothing more than a form of narcissistic pain.

It was Stella's choice to do something about her issues and the situation our relationship was in, as well as to choose to work together to see if things could be improved. She chose to run away and re-establish her life with someone else in a completely different environment.

The opportunity to face up to her issues with my loving support was simply not valued.

Nothing Can Save Us Now

My letter to Stella was a complete failure. She saw it as completely blaming her for the state of our marriage. To her, it was full of negative comments and vitriol.

Towards the end of our time together, when Stella came back from a trip interstate and told me that our marriage was over, I actually agreed with her and told her that this was what I also wanted. There was absolutely no buy-in on her behalf to getting professional help or taking a step back to objectively look at what I had written in my letter.

I left the house in a state of bewilderment and spent the night at a friend's place.

The next morning when I went home, Stella was adamant that our marriage was finished. I told her that I was still going to see the psychologist to talk about the issues she had with me, and that I hoped she would change her mind and join me in seeking professional help to try and save our marriage.

* * *

In order to attempt to save our relationship I did arrange to see a psychologist.

As requested by Stella, I took my final letter to the psychologist, as well as fulfilling her request to ask the psychologist why I had deliberately and intentionally not looked after any of her needs throughout the entire relationship.

By this stage I was beside myself with anxiety. I knew that Stella's question was simply ridiculous. I was determined to do all I could, and was open to putting everything on the table for discussion, review, and change.

The beginning of my meeting with the psychologist had the usual awkwardness that you would expect. I was asked the usual questions as to why I was meeting with her, and was also asked to describe a little bit about myself, as well as my family and upbringing.

I mentioned that I was there to try and save my marriage, and that my wife had requested I ask the psychologist a certain question, and show her the letter that I had written to my wife.

I asked the psychologist to take things slowly and not to jump to too many conclusions about Stella without having met her. My preference was for me to meet with her first, for Stella to then join in the process separately, and for us to then attend joint relationship counselling sessions.

This was agreed with the psychologist. I then told her about my unconditionally loving upbringing and childhood, as well as the beautiful parents I was lucky enough to have been raised by. I remember the psychologist telling me my description of my upbringing and childhood was beautifully expressed and one of the best she had heard. I also elaborated on how I saw myself as a parent to my own children, with the ability to remember and reflect back on myself now being the age of my parents. I recalled the way they handled me and my siblings, given the different circumstances and changes to expectations that had taken place between the different generations. I mentioned that I could easily see and identify my parenting shortcomings with regard to my children.

From there it was down to business. I was a little emotional, and obviously upset by all that was happening with my marriage and my family.

At the request of the psychologist, I then asked her the question that Stella had requested I ask.

I felt silly asking this question, and a little awkward. The psychologist immediately put this question to one side, seemed a tad taken aback, and said she would deal with it a little later. I was then asked to show her a copy of the letter I had written to Stella.

The psychologist excused herself and took my letter into another room to read. About ten minutes later she returned with a rather concerned look and sat down opposite me. From there, I was asked a number of questions, including whether I had written the letter and how long it had taken.

I confirmed that I had written the letter, that it had taken about half an hour, and that it had been written straight from the heart with absolutely no ill intent.

She told me that my letter was beautifully written. 'Any emotionally stable woman would be delighted to receive a letter like this from their partner,' she said. 'It contains no blame, no malice, no disrespect, or ill intent. It simply describes where you see your marriage, a sensible way forward, and your complete buy-in to try and save your marriage with a person you clearly love and value very highly.'

I was absolutely delighted to hear the psychologist had interpreted my letter to Stella in this way.

From this point, things were tactfully handled by the psychologist. I asked if she thought there was a spectrum issue. She asked what I meant by that. I had been doing some reading on toxic relationships, and all the psychological and emotional issues that come with conditions such as bipolar disorder, borderline personality disorder (BPD), narcissistic personality disorder (NPD), depression, and so on.

The psychologist took my lead here, and said that there were many issues in my letter and that she believed none of them were to do with me. We then talked a little further about BPD. Down the track the psychologist told me that she wanted to tell me there and then that my letter had unknowingly, almost perfectly, described narcissism, and that Stella, from what I had described, was easily one of the top half a dozen people of this type of person that she had encountered. Needless to say I was taken aback by all of this.

From the first session with the psychologist I came to understand many things, including:

1   Our marriage was in a perilous state. I thought I was dealing with someone with BPD but it was in fact NPD, as I was later to discover.

2   The issues were largely not to do with me. I remember feeling a great sense of relief to be told this, as I also felt that this was the case.

3   The psychologist told me to turn my mobile back on, as she was certain that I would receive a call from Stella as soon as she thought my session with the psychologist had ended. We went overtime deliberately by about five minutes, and my mobile did ring. As instructed, I didn't answer the call. It was no surprise to the psychologist that it was Stella. The psychologist explained that Stella would want to know what the psychologist had said to me, both about the question I had been directed by Stella to ask, as well as their professional opinion of the letter I had written. The psychologist said that Stella would need immediate confirmation and validation that I was the one at fault, the one who needed to change, and that I had let her down badly. Given Stella's earlier counselling sessions, this all sounded very familiar.

4   A further understanding that this meeting gave me was that the psychologist thought I demonstrated that I was in a very fragile, psychological state, and was more than likely suffering from Post-Traumatic Stress Disorder (PTSD). I was also taken aback by this, and found it a little offensive, as I thought this type of disorder was something that returned soldiers developed. The psychologist, who happened to specialise in NPD, said I had very much been involved in a war with Stella.

5   The final thing I got out of the initial meeting was that I needed to have quite a few more sessions to deal with my distress, to try and save my marriage, and to get my thinking back on to a more even keel. My psychologist said that our marriage could be saved, but that it would come at a cost to me. The cost would involve being caught up in a somewhat emotionless and shallow relationship that would be almost entirely about giving to my partner, with very little emotional support, understanding, true love, or empathy in return. I was simply blown away by this thought.

On reflection, my final letter to Stella marked the end of our marriage. As previously discussed, it was a genuine last-ditch attempt to save our marriage and to move forward with renewed understanding, albeit without me knowing with what I was dealing.

The psychologist later explained to me that a letter of the type I had written to Stella, who she believed to be suffering from NPD, would have represented what is called a 'narcissistic injury' to Stella. A narcissistic injury is a perceived threat to a narcissist's self-esteem or self-worth.

To Stella, the letter was like putting the spotlight on her. I had identified her issues without knowing it. I think she was becoming uncomfortable with me piecing things together. She was not going to be able to manipulate me anymore. Her issues were now on the table.

It was her choice to do something about the situation, and to seek to change. She could do something about herself, with my support, or simply run away again and look to continue her life with someone else.

I left my first session with the psychologist feeling much better about myself, feeling far better informed about what I was dealing with but, nevertheless, clueless about what I was going to do moving forward, and all the time battling away with a very fragile state of mind. Things were not looking good for us.

I think this first session marked the beginning of a very short 'push the delete button' phase of our relationship. There was to be no buy-in whatsoever from Stella, even though I tried to raise things in a very sensitive and caring way.

The psychologist later said to me that due to the way Stella had conveniently misinterpreted my letter, it had effectively ended our marriage.

'You, in fact, left Stella, and not the other way around,' she said.

Stage Three:

Push the Delete
Button Phase

The Last Throes

This phase of our relationship was brief, perhaps even brutal. In Stella's mind, now was the time to leave our marriage and family, and continue her life with her children and a new partner. For Stella, I think the 'push the delete button' phase lasted no longer than it took to remove her possessions from the marital home.

I was still hoping that things could be worked out between us and that we could move on with renewed understandings, with the help of individual and couples counselling.

With my feelings of anxiety at heightened levels, and clueless about Stella's commitment to our relationship, I tried to discuss with Stella the outcomes of my initial meeting with my psychologist.

In this process I naively mentioned the conversation that I had raised with the psychologist about borderline personality disorder. Although I say I raised this issue naively, I knew that it would not go down well if Stella was not going to accept the possibility that her issues were playing a major role in the state of our relationship.

Once Stella realised that the psychologist was talking about her she blew up. She shutdown, her eyes glazed over, and I prepared myself for yet another tirade. It didn't happen, but I knew that our relationship and marriage had more than likely reached a point of no return.

Stella exclaimed that the psychologist has not met her, which was fair enough. The bottom line, though, was that it was very clear that she was not going to take ownership for being in any way responsible or accountable for the state of our marriage. In her mind, the fact that I was willing to see the psychologist meant that the issues affecting our relationship in such a negative way were all mine, and so it was down to me to take full responsibility for them and make the necessary changes.

Offering to see the psychologist, as an individual or with me, was not something she was prepared to do.

* * *

At the second meeting with my psychologist I talked about the discussion with Stella and reported that she had said our marriage was over. I was not in a great state of mind, and my psychologist tried to get me back on an even keel.

After about half a dozen sessions my psychologist made the decision that I was in a stable enough state of mind to hear the assessment from my initial meeting that was actually the truth, from their viewpoint.

The psychologist read out a paper on the three stages of a narcissistic relationship and told me that this was what I had been through and that, from looking at Stella's public social media accounts, she thought that Stella was comfortably within the top half a dozen narcissists she had ever seen in all her years of professional practice. I was somewhat comforted by this assessment, and remember feeling that a great weight was lifted off my shoulders. The psychologist's assessment was the logical answer to the emotional turmoil I was living with externally, as well as within.

I knew the problems with our relationship and marriage were largely not to do with me.

I saw my psychologist several more times, and I was told what to expect from Stella now that our relationship was over.

These things included the expectation to see increasingly desperate and erratic behaviour from Stella, as well as no ownership or responsibility for her actions and behaviours, with the understanding that narcissistic people do not have normal emotions, even towards their own children, and little or no ability to feel empathy.

All of this did happen. I now finally knew and accepted what I had been dealing with since I had met Stella. I further understood that her psychological and emotional issues had been skilfully hidden from me prior to our marriage.

Although deeply affected by the relationship breakdown, to my psychologist's surprise I got my act together before the need to start a cognitive behaviour therapy program. I credit this to the conversations I had with people who opened up to me about their experiences with Stella, and told me that they had heard all of this before and that it was not my fault. Being told by a professional that Stella suffers from NPD was also significant. Even so, the road to recovery was still long and difficult.

*** * ***

We were done. Stella made this very clear. However, the psychologist had made it clear to me that she would not entertain the idea of any joint counselling with me and Stella. Her view was that Stella would have to come to the conclusion that she needed to get help before anyone would be able to attempt to help her with her significant and entrenched psychological and emotional issues. It was the opinion of my psychologist that Stella would not have the foresight to seek sustained professional help. Communication between Stella and me was awful.

Through this period of time, I was unaware that Stella was already in the process of seeking a rental property in order to leave our home. In her mind she now had no choice. She expressed the view to me that I had left her no choice and that I was throwing her out on the street because I would not leave the house with my children. She told people that she had to leave quickly because she felt under threat. In my opinion, all of this was about her protecting her image, and nothing more than that. I accept it would have been true in her mind at the time.

*** * ***

This occasion was absolutely crazy.

Stella gave me the impression that she had decided we were done. She was involved on a committee that was running a fundraising event at the local sporting club and asked that I contact former neighbours to come with us to the event and to stay overnight at our place. I was also to inform our neighbours that we were separating. This all made no sense to me.

Before our neighbours turned up, Stella asked me to take a picture of her in her gown, which was inevitably going to be immediately posted on social media. I took six pictures before she was happy, and she then posted the picture on social media to receive back the instant 'Likes'. I was then asked to rub fake tan on her back.

On a number of occasions, I was also asked if I thought she looked pretty in her dress. The wife of our mutual friends later remarked that Stella's dress and appearance was more akin to an A-lister going to the Academy Awards than someone attending a fundraising night at the local sporting club. It all looked way over-the-top.

Our neighbours turned up and, after a short conversation, Stella headed up to the local sporting club to meet and greet people at the door.

This was a chance for our neighbours and friends to talk with me, which I really appreciated. Our neighbours said that they did not see this coming, and that it might be best for me if I did not come with them to the event.

I thanked them and said I would go for the meal and, if things were proving too difficult for me, I would leave and come home. I also said that I wanted to go and support Stella, and thought it was the right thing to do. To be truthful, I was also hopeful of Stella changing her mind with her decision to end our relationship.

I arrived at the function with our neighbours. Stella was at the door, being her usual happy, excited, fun-loving public self. I was warmly greeted with a hug and a kiss from Stella, as though she was my very loving wife, and that we were a very happily married couple. I set about mingling among the many people I knew, determined to have a reasonable time.

Once Stella had finished with her greeting duties she came over and joined me with a group of friends. She quietly asked me a number of questions, such as, 'Do you think I look pretty?', 'Do you still love me?', and, 'Are people looking at me?'

In response to the last question I could see that people in the room were looking at Stella, and taking note of her over-the-top dress. The men might have been thinking that she looked alright, and the women thinking that she was overdressed for the occasion.

Perhaps they were even wondering, '*Who does she think she is? A princess?*'

We sat down for our meal and I tried my best to keep things normal and engage in conversation with those around the table. Nothing seemed out of the ordinary. I doubt anyone knew, other than our neighbours, that our marriage was over. Stella then lent over towards me and, again, asked the same questions as to whether I loved her, did I think she looked pretty, and did I like her dress. Then a final question that made me leave the table and go home.

As Stella lent over towards me she pulled her dress top slightly away from her chest and asked me if I thought the pattern around her bra matched her dress. This was enough for me and, having eaten my meal, I told Stella that I was going home.

Once home I was too embarrassed to sleep where I usually slept, because our neighbours were staying over, so I slept in one of my children's rooms. Upon returning home with the neighbours, Stella went from room to room yelling out with an almost comical voice of concern and asking where I was. It was crazy stuff.

Next morning I got up early to prepare some breakfast for the neighbours. Stella came down and I thought I greeted her appropriately. The neighbours soon left, after what must have been an awkward night for them. Stella then proceeded to complain to me about a number of things that she did not approve of, including the way I had greeted her in front of the neighbours that morning.

The neighbours later told me that there was nothing wrong with what I had done and that they thought I had done more than could have been expected of me under the extremely difficult circumstances I was dealing with.

* * *

Things were really crazy in our household by this time. Stella had found somewhere else to live, and was setting about packing up her things and taking them to her new place. I was in a state of absolute anxiety and devastation. One minute Stella would shower with me, and in the next moment I would be accused of making her feel unsafe.

On this particular occasion I entered the ensuite in an attempt to talk to Stella about what was going on. She backed away from me. I believe she thought I was going to harm her in some way. In backing away she clipped her ankle on the edge of the bath, and then accused me of pushing her.

Stella then raced down stairs and, in a highly agitated and anxious state, said she was going to call the police. It was yet another ridiculous situation. Our children were home at the time. I had followed her downstairs and said to her that what she had convinced herself of having happened had not, in fact, happened. I had not touched Stella. I said to her that the children were in the house and that calling the police was not in their best interests. They did not need to be caught up in this.

Stella processed what I said. She had effectively had another emotional meltdown. Her 'pig eyes' were present, and I could see her processing the events as well as the insanity of what she was considering doing. Once again, this was all about Stella looking to manufacture a convenient excuse for her unbalanced actions and behaviours.

Thankfully, this incident passed without the children knowing and the police not being involved. I stayed well away from Stella from then on, and let her go about packing up her things to leave. It was an incredibly sad and distressing time.

This incident was one of a number in the last few weeks where Stella could turn without warning and accuse me of behaviour that just wasn't happening but seemed very real to her. I was accused of standing over her as she lay in her bed, and of blocking the exit for her from a room, the ensuite, or the laundry. This simply was not the case. On no occasion, when Stella took this tack, did I deny that what she was thinking was not the reality, and move to let her leave the room on her terms. I remember her saying to me that I was good at intimidating people and making out I was not.

* * *

This particular incident happened in the very last days. With Stella telling me that she was leaving, I reclaimed the main bedroom and told Stella that she could sleep out in the family area, as I had done for the past three or four years. She, of course, rejected this request, but I made it clear to her that she was not going to be welcome in the main bedroom under the current circumstances. It was also easier for me to have the main bedroom, as I left earlier for work and could shower and get dressed without disturbing the household.

By this stage I was wracked with anxiety, completely bewildered by what Stella was doing, and physically, emotionally, and psychologically exhausted. Looking for peace, quiet, and rest, I went to bed about 8.30pm. I was about to lie down when Stella came through the double doors and, in her usual vile tone and aggressive manner, said, 'Look at you now. It's 8.30pm and you are going to bed! What are you? Eighty years old or something? This is another reason why I am leaving you!'

I told her that I would like her to leave the room and that I was exhausted and needed to rest. Her retort was that I was 'fucking weird'. She then went on about me wanting to sleep in the bedroom with the curtains open while downstairs I wanted them shut. I told her that upstairs, when she was not in the room, I liked to sleep with the curtains open but had always compromised on her need to have them closed. Downstairs, I thought we had agreed they should be closed at night for privacy reasons, as well as to keep the heat within the house when the heating was on and it was cold.

Stella then moved towards me in an aggressive fashion. I could see she was trying to provoke me to do something that was inappropriate. I clasped my hands together and placed them behind my back. Stella then moved into my personal space and, with her thumb and forefinger next to each other, about an inch apart, placed them under my nose and in an awful and aggressive tone said, 'You are within one inch of violence aren't you, you bastard!'

I stepped away in a state of disbelief. Stella then pulled down her pants, kicked off her underwear and placed them in the laundry basket, pulled her pants back up and left the room calling me a 'fucking weirdo'.

I was relieved when Stella left the room. All of this from a person who said she felt unsafe around me, who continued to feel the need to be naked around me, and was actually in the process of leaving me.

What more can I say? What I witnessed were extremely provocative actions and behaviours.

* * *

At the time of this particular incident, Stella had packed and moved a reasonable portion of her belongings to her new rental property. She had already expressed the view to me, in a rather aggressive fashion, that I had not even helped her pack. This staggered me. I didn't want her to leave. I think that statement was, once again, about not wanting to be involved in another failed marriage, trying to protect all the children, pure emotional and psychological exhaustion, and a sense of naïve optimism that Stella would finally come to her senses and get the professional help I thought she needed.

Within days of leaving, as I was again trying to talk to her about what was happening, Stella turned to me and in her usual aggressive and nasty tone accused me of making her sell her washing machine, bed, dryer, and fridge. This was all completely insane.

Selling and giving Stella's things away when we moved in together was a joint decision at the time. We got rid of items that were no longer required and kept those that were in better working order. It was the sensible thing to do. Stella claiming I had forced her to get rid of her things was totally discarding any responsibility or accountability for being very much a part of these decisions. She was now looking to play the victim. Pathetic stuff.

In the end, to resolve this situation, it was agreed between us to advance a significant amount of money to Stella, against her equity in the house, to purchase any new items she needed. This advance of equity was given in good faith by me, to help alleviate her distress, but with the understanding that it was to be either repaid or considered as being part of her equity split. In the final settlement, she refused to repay the money or have it considered as being part of her final equity in the house proceeds.

* * *

Looking back, this incident was completely bizarre. It was about six o' clock in the morning, and I was lying in bed in the main bedroom. Suddenly, the doors opened and in came Stella carrying her pillow and wearing very little. She then, to my bewilderment, proceeded to get into the bed with me and asked me to hold and hug her. She stayed with me for about forty-five minutes, before leaving and beginning her day. I was completely confused. Yet again, I asked her not to leave. To this day I do not know if what Stella did was her handing out more cruelty to me, not wanting to go, being scared, saying sorry to me for all the pain she had caused, or simply wanting some attention. I have no idea, and found it most unusual and, in hindsight, very sad.

* * *

On the evening of the day that Stella got into bed with me, we each unknowingly took our children to the same local eatery for tea. The situation was a little awkward and, after a while, I went over to Stella's table and asked her children to join mine so I could have one last chat with her. I once again expressed the view that I didn't want her to leave and hoped that we could work it all out. All of a sudden Stella's mood changed and she said to me in the usual awful tone that I had loved her with malice and neglect. I simply couldn't believe what she had said, let alone understand why she had said it. Can you even love someone with malice?

That night we all went back to our house and went to bed. I was the last person to find out that Stella had booked a removalist truck for the next morning. She had told her children, who had told mine, and the night before the truck arrived I was told by my children. It was devastating for me.

On that last night, one of my children was extremely upset, and I asked Stella to leave her room and let me deal with it. My child cried for a good thirty minutes, absolutely devastated by Stella's decision to leave our family. Later that night I took the opportunity to explain to Stella that the emotions she witnessed were genuine, and those of a child who cared for, trusted, and loved her as a stepmother. This was something that I suspected Stella as an NPD sufferer, as I had been professionally informed she was, couldn't actually understand or feel. It was an incredibly sad, yet enlightening, conversation for me to have with Stella. She simply didn't understand the feelings that my children had for her, because they were not expressed towards her in the unfortunate ways that she had experienced in her childhood years.

* * *

The next morning, I got up and prepared myself for work, knowing that a removalist truck was coming and that my marriage was over. It was surreal. I got myself dressed and went out into the family area where Stella had slept. She was awake. I took the opportunity to lie down next to her and appealed to her not to leave. She said that it was too late.

I then gave her a kiss on the cheek, and remember looking up at her as I walked down the stairs to the front door as she calmly folded some towels. I said, 'So I just go to work then, and that's it?'

That night I came home to a half empty house, and Stella and her children were gone. It was over. I remember walking through the house with my children, and I think we were all very sad, if not a little shell-shocked. I still had to carry on and get my children some tea. I remember having to go up to the local shopping centre to get another frying pan, as Stella had taken mine and refused to give it back.

Within a short time of Stella leaving she said the following gems, 'When I left you and that family, within two days I was able to stop taking all my supplements.' And, 'You better keep that house clean and presentable as I will not be coming around with a bucket and a mop to clean up after you and your children.'

Unbelievable, really. There is not much more to say. Stella appeared to have disconnected from our marriage and family with the ease of someone who had very little emotional skin in the game.

Within a couple of days I was told by mutual friends that Stella had changed her social media status to single, and blocked many people who were a part of our lives, including my children. There was to be no counselling or chance for reconciliation. One of her emails to me did say that she had explained her issues with me thousands of times. With the preface that I consider myself to be far from perfect, and not without fault, through all Stella's tantrums, emotional meltdowns, and tirades, there were never any real clear messages, apart from her claiming that I was totally responsible and accountable for her ongoing unhappiness. Other people we knew came to the same conclusion.

So ended the 'push the delete button' phase of my marriage to Stella.

The Aftermath

Picking Up the Pieces

For the first couple of weeks after Stella left, I was in a shocked and stunned state of mind. I simply couldn't believe that she had moved out and left our marriage without any counselling or attempt to clearly explain her issues and try to save our relationship.

It was in about the third or fourth session with the psychologist that I was told that I had most definitely married a narcissist.

Once I was told this, a huge weight came off my shoulders. That moment was pivotal in my recovery, as was talking to a number of people who were aware of the type of person Stella was.

I was very grateful for the time I spent with my psychologist, who fortunately specialised in narcissists. However, it was one thing to finally know what I had been dealing with, and still very much another to accept and recover from the experience.

The honest truth is that it took a good six months for me to work my way through the mental fog that had descended upon me. I sank to new lows in my life. I simply could not believe that I had been so fooled by the act and display that Stella had put on for me during our courtship.

My road to recovery involved antidepressant and anxiety medications, regular appointments with my psychologist, and the wonderful support of my family and children. My employer was also incredibly supportive, as were my work colleagues. I was determined to move on with my life, get past this experience, and implement a number of changes.

Aside from seeing my psychologist for another couple of months, I wrote down a number of thoughts that I carried around with me in my wallet and read them out in times of sadness, depression, and doubt. I called this my 'Daily Mantra'.

Here are the things I would quietly read and say to myself:

1. She is a narcissist. Get over the shock of finding that out.

2. You are well rid of her.

3. Stop giving her the power of your pain and wasting your emotional energy on her.

4. Accept that it is over and that she was very bad for you.

5. As far as my future is concerned, she is to be treated as deceased.

6. She did not love you and played happy families.

7. She is a false, fake, and plastic person.

8. You did genuinely love her, presented yourself honestly, and tried your best to make it work.

9. Happiness awaits you, choose to seek it now.

I lost count of the number of times I read this list over the horrible six-month period I struggled through during this lowest period of my life.

I also decided to write down four or five things that I was going to do, or had always wanted to do, and did them. This helped greatly in my recovery, with one of the things on my bucket list being to write a book.

In spite of my efforts to move on, I had not fully accepted the breakdown of my marriage to Stella and tried my best to win her back. I tried to leave her alone for periods and wrote to her, all the while knowing that it was futile. It was a very confusing, distressing, emotional, and upsetting time for me. In the back of my mind, and armed with the knowledge and understanding that Stella suffered from NPD, I still wanted to think that I could fix things, help her find herself, and get our marriage and family back together again.

After a couple of months apart, and still with some sort of hope that we could get back together again, I agreed to meet Stella at a local restaurant to have a meal and discuss, I thought, where things were at with us. This was after Stella had informed me that she could not fit our meeting into her diary for three weeks, as she was so busy.

Obviously, the priority of putting our marriage and family back together was not high on her agenda. Before this meeting I specifically told her that I did not want to meet her if discussing our reconciliation was not a priority for her.

With high hopes I met her at the local restaurant, and received what seemed like a warm welcome. We were seated with a nice glass of wine, and our meals were ordered. Conversation was relatively easy, given the awkward circumstances, and our meals arrived within a relatively short time.

At this stage I still naively thought that Stella and I could work out our issues, albeit with significant professional assistance. I also think that I hadn't fully accepted the extent of her emotional and psychological issues. Foolishly, I thought that she may have had time to reflect on things and want to come back.

Stella seemed preoccupied with a situation with one of her children and their father. She had instructed the child to ring her immediately if they felt unsafe, and she would then go and 'rescue' them. The possibility of police involvement was also mentioned. As a result, Stella was constantly looking at her mobile. Knowing the father and the child involved, the whole situation seemed rather exaggerated, over the top, and a tad manipulative.

At one point during our conversation, Stella said that her life wasn't very good at the moment, and that she had been working very hard to re-establish herself. On top of our divorce, things were a little difficult. I think she may have forgotten herself here, and I immediately interrupted her train of thought to remind her that I had specifically said that, if this meeting was not about talking about our reconciliation, then I did not want to attend. Stella then confirmed that she did want a divorce. I stood up and calmly told her I was leaving, that I was very disappointed in what she had said, and that I wished her all the best.

Stella was left to pay the bill.

* * *

Walking back to my car I made a very conscious effort to finally let go of Stella and completely accept the advice of my psychologist that I would better off with her out of my life. Friends and family also backed up this view.

From this point forward I quickly moved to dismantle our finances and carry out various repairs on our marital home in order to place it on the market. Engaging a solicitor to formalise our property split was also a high priority.

I dismantled our financial affairs in a considerate, fair, and professional manner. Of course, none of this was to Stella's liking. I was simply not adhering to her timetable, and she had lost control of the situation.

I gave Stella plenty of notice about changing her health care cover before I removed her and her children from our family cover. The proposed split was explained and discussed by email with both Stella and her lawyer. The opportunity for Stella to take over the payment of her personal insurance covers, before they lapsed through non-payment, was also made. Although I was somewhat reluctant to have this happen, I also agreed to have Stella arrange for some renovations to our martial home before placing it on the market.

In this process, having moved away from the marital home, I spent many hours fixing up the home for sale, as well as going to the house before and after each open, to ensure it was presentable.

Apart from arranging for the renovations she wanted, and Stella taking responsibility for engaging an agent to sell the home, her other contribution was to do a final clean of the home, before the settlement. I considered this to be completely unnecessary, as the home had been professionally cleaned, including the carpets, and I saw this as a sort of final attempt by her to exercise control. She had to contribute in some way, to make herself feel happy. Perhaps this need to do the final clean also fits in with the disgraceful thing Stella said to me, in the usual vile and aggressive tone, not long after she left, about not coming around with a mop and a bucket to clean up after me and my children.

With regard to the formal and legal property settlement process, I acknowledge that this process can be very difficult, and often nasty. Ours seemed to go relatively smoothly, but not without some difficulty.

I was particularly taken aback by a written request from her lawyer with regard to requiring a greater split of the equity than was proposed, based on the 'non-financial' things she had done for my children.

I was absolutely staggered by this request. My reply was to ask her to state how much more of the equity she wished to receive, as well as an explanation of the formula used for each of my children and an explanation of the difference, if there was any, between each of my children.

I also told Stella my thoughts with regard to any additional equity coming to me for all the 'non-financial' things I had done for her children during the marriage and family times we had together. After a minuscule time of consideration, I asked for $0 of increased equity for each of her children. I stated that I did not feel the need to explain the basis of any formula in my claim, because it amounted to $0. I ended by saying that it was my privilege to have had them in my life, and that they would all be sadly missed.

How do you put a monetary value on this type of thing? Stella's request more or less ties in with what my psychologist said to me in regard to NPD sufferers not being able to feel the love and empathy for other people that normal people feel.

She was simply acting and putting on a display.

Collateral Damage

There is just one final point that I would like to note.

It is a very sensitive area, to do with the way Stella interacted with her children. Many other people commented on the unusual relationship that Stella had with her children. They almost always mentioned Stella's relationship with her children as being 'over the top', as demonstrated by her social media posts, professing to the world how much she loved them. Everyone seemed to question, as I did, why this needed to be done. The vast majority of parents love their children. That is a normal feeling. Why do you need to tell your children that you love them through social media? Who are you trying to convince? The children? Yourself? Or others?

Without doubt, all of us pass on a mixture of the positive and the negative parenting that we experienced in our own childhoods. Stella was no different in this regard. In my view, some of the negative parenting that Stella obviously experienced in her upbringing were abnormally passed on to her children.

What I regularly observed with Stella in her daily interactions with her children was her perceived pain and issues with people in her life being transferred onto her children. Her children were not given the space, time, or ability to grow or mature to a point where they could form their own untainted views of other people in their lives.

Stella would colour her children's views of other people in their lives by a number of methods. When her children's behaviour towards other people was not respectful, this did not result in appropriate correction or discipline. In fact, there was almost an encouragement by Stella of their disrespect towards certain people. It was the way she felt about these people, so it must also be the way her children felt. This occurred on numerous occasions. There was also great restriction of her children's opportunity to interact with certain people, simply because Stella didn't want to have any interaction with them herself. The payment of an excessive amount of pocket money was also a lure to have her children gravitate towards her.

Even though Stella's children were relatively young, they seemed to know that things would be best for them if they more or less accepted their mother's views. A former work colleague backed up this view. In adulthood, they came to realise that they had grown up in an environment where they were raised by a single, narcissistic parent. They describe their childhood as effectively being used as a prop by the parent. Love was conditional. They acted out, being and saying what they thought the parent wanted them to. It was easiest that way, especially when others were around. They came to realise quite early that all of this was for the self-gratification of their parent.

Stella's children were also made to be aware of the difference in the money between our household and that of their father. They also knew what they needed to do to fill their mother's love tanks, and the rewards that they would get when they did. It was all quite unhealthy to me, and to many other people. Although she gave to her children, in fact she probably spoiled them, it seemed as though they needed to give her more back than the norm for her to feel good about herself.

With our marriage having now split up, my psychologist told me that Stella would be searching for another 'source of supply.' Until she found a new partner this was likely to be her children. Based on her posts on social media, it looked as though she had already set up a new relationship before she left our marriage. All standard stuff for NPD sufferers.

With regard to her children, I was stunned to receive a number of texts from one of them that effectively demonstrates my point.

These texts came without warning, and were from a relatively young child who should not have had the type of thoughts expressed.

The comments were expletive laden, contained threats of violence against me, and were filled with adult themes as well as derogatory comments. The child involved had obviously had a great deal of information about our relationship and failed marriage downloaded onto them by their mother.

This was all incredibly sad to me, as it was highly inappropriate. I reacted by replying to the texts to Stella, the child involved, and the child's father, and asked that he intervene to stop any further messages being sent. I could not imagine my own children thinking that way, let alone sending texts of that nature to Stella. If they had there would have been reasonably severe consequences for them. I gave the child concerned the benefit of the doubt.

Was it Stella using their mobile, or maybe a collaborative effort? Regardless, the messages were inappropriate, and a clear example to me of one of her children being used as a source of supply.

This text exchange marked the end for me. I simply wanted Stella out of my life as soon as possible.

The Quotes

What I would like to do now is explain the circumstances around a number of things that Stella said to me, primarily after we married.

These quotes, in a way, tell the story of my experience, and will be put in a rough chronological order. This may seem like a little bit of a strange thing to do and you may well be asking why I would remember these things. I remember them because they were things that were said to me by Stella in such a toxic and aggressive tone during her tantrums, emotional meltdowns, and tirades. The things said were so far beyond the norm, were rarely, if ever, apologised for, and were incredibly damaging to me. They are burnt into my brain. It was unlike anything I had experienced in any other relationship.

When I reflect back upon these quotes, I think of two things.

The first is that they seemed to have been said by a disordered, emotional person. They seem to be said by someone who is emotionally unhinged. Why would anyone think it was appropriate to speak to their partner in this way?

Secondly, there was no reflection after the comments were made. No apology. In the moment they were said I am sure they were the truth to Stella. She actually believed that was she was saying was right. She was protecting herself, in her mind, and standing up for herself. To a certain extent I think she knew what she was saying, but she also knew that what she was saying was not balanced. She needed to lash out, blame, and make me responsible for her deep feelings of unhappiness. It was crazy to be on the receiving end of these comments, and very damaging to my sense of self, no matter how strong that may have been.

The reality is that if the majority of these things had been said to me by Stella before we married, I would not have asked her to marry me.

What follows are some of the comments that I remember Stella making to me, and my response to what was said with the benefit of hindsight.

'He is my soulmate.'

This comment was made to my mother fairly early on in our relationship. No doubt this comment was part of the process that Stella used to win over family members. My mother never told me about what Stella said, until after our marriage had failed.

'You married a broken person who never really committed emotionally to the marriage.'

Where is the ownership of her actions and behaviours in marrying me in the first place if this was how she felt?

'You didn't even carry me into the room on our wedding night.'

This comment was made after our marriage failed. I simply failed to live up to Stella's 'Mills & Boon' notion of a romantic wedding night. I didn't carry her into our room. I failed to read her mind or to realise that this was what she wanted me to do. Running a spa and sharing a glass of champagne just didn't cut it. In hindsight, this was a disastrous start to our marriage and effectively the beginning of the end.

'You didn't even give me a hug on our first Christmas.'

This comment was also made after our marriage failed. Apparently, on our first Christmas Day together, I failed to give her a hug. This went straight into her Vault of Resentment, and was subsequently carried from that point forward for the entire marriage. What I remember of our first Christmas Day together is working flat out to entertain and provide for both of our families. I thought it was a great day. If Stella wanted a hug that badly, why didn't she simply ask me for one, or come up and give me one?

'How many of your children's Christmas presents have you wrapped?'

Christmas for Stella was an extravaganza. It was always about Stella putting on an event or a display that was over the top. It was yet another example of her need to overcompensate for what she felt she didn't get from her own childhood.

I hadn't helped Stella wrap the presents. Once again, what I did was not good enough in her eyes. I was caught out again. If I helped, I knew what I did wouldn't be good enough. If I didn't help then it would be stored away in the Vault of Resentment to be blurted out at a later date. I simply couldn't win.

'Pleading the fifth again, are you?'

This was a standard remark that Stella made on many occasions when she had manipulated a situation to the point that I could not answer her next question without being guilty of letting her down in some way. There was nothing I could say or do, or not say or do, that would be satisfactory to her as a response. It was like a crowning moment for her. If I tried to respond, no matter how logical the response, she took the position that I was being manipulative. If I didn't respond I was admitting my guilt or wrong-doing.

'I will give our marriage my all.'

This comment was said to me on a number of occasions. I am sure that she would claim she did give our marriage her all, but how can you say this when you admit that you had made no emotional commitment to the marriage whatsoever? To me, no emotional commitment means no marriage.

'You loved me with malice, you loved me with neglect, you are an arrogant man, and you are an alpha male.'

These are accusations that Stella regularly shouted at me during her tantrums, emotional meltdowns, and tirades. I think they may have come about because I didn't completely yield to her need for power and control over me and challenged her to get some professional help with her obvious personal issues. None of them really make any sense. I am not sure how you can love someone with malice and neglect. My psychologist didn't assess me as being 'an arrogant man' or 'an alpha male'.

'This is how hard I have tried to feel a part of this family.'

This statement occurred at the bottom of the stairs when Stella showed me a Life Tree and a heart-shaped gathering of a number of pictures of us looking happy. Once again, it all made little sense to me. The happiness for me was in my mind and heart. I didn't need to have this type of reminder around the house to try and feel something or demonstrate to myself how hard I had tried to be a part of our family.

'You stopped me from dancing around the kitchen table!'
'You stopped me from playing music!'
'You made me sell my washing machine!'
'You made me sell my bed!'
'You made me sell my dryer!'
'You made me sell my fridge!'
'You didn't even leave me a broom!'

These remarks, made to me in the usual aggressive and toxic fashion, were said towards the end of our time living together. They had no basis of truth to me at all. I most certainly did not stop her from dancing around the kitchen table or playing music. These were baseless and ridiculous claims. I am sure that to Stella they were true. The other comments also had no basis in truth. Selling her furniture and household goods was discussed and agreed upon when we moved in to our home together. It made sense as the items were surplus to our requirements, and my furniture and household goods were more modern. Not leaving her with a broom was a victim-like statement that I had left her with nothing and was forcing her out of the house. Simply not the case.

'You have not even helped me pack.'

This comment came as she systematically packed up all her belongings and those of her children and prepared to leave our marital home. I didn't help her pack, and chose to try and stay out of her way. At the time I think I was in some sort of shock with regard to what I was witnessing. My anxiety levels were extremely high. I was trying to talk to her. I didn't want her to leave. I was shocked that she was leaving and that she had leased a rental property for a twelve-month period. I wanted us to at least undertake some counselling together to try and save our marriage. Nothing was making any sense to me at this time. Stella was practically impossible to approach and unable to discuss things in a calm, reasonable, and rational frame of mind.

'You're within one inch of violence, aren't you, you bastard.'

This awful comment was screamed at me in the scene that occurred in the main bedroom at the very end of our time living together. Simply untrue. I am not a violent man. Stella, in fact, was lucky that I was not a violent man. On this particular occasion she most certainly did her very best to be provocative and bait me to be violent towards her and therefore give her the excuse she needed to justify her unbalanced actions and behaviours.

I had left her no choice, and was effectively throwing her out on the street because I **'would not leave the house with my children'** and she told people that she had to leave quickly because she felt **'under threat'**.

Just a couple of 'Stella Facts' here, and simply not true in either case. Stella chose to leave. She and her children were not thrown out onto the street. She left once a satisfactory rental had been leased. I did not want her to go. I was devastated when she did and, as previously mentioned, the last to know that she had booked a removalist truck.

Telling others that she had to leave quickly because she felt under threat was a lie. I am sure that she felt she was under threat but it simply was not the case. For starters, all our children were living in the house at the time she left. Her thoughts of feeling under threat were very convenient. At no time did Stella feel threatened to the extent that she felt the need to leave the house and go to stay with her mother, a friend, a sibling, or even book herself into a motel. This claim was about her image protection, and a justification in her mind of her erratic and unbalanced actions and behaviours.

'When I left you and that family I stopped taking all my supplements within two days'

This was said to me by Stella within days of leaving and was just a horrible thing to say. It demonstrates to me that she had no 'skin in the game', no empathy, and placed no value whatsoever on our relationship, marriage, or family. All of a sudden 'our family' became 'you and that family.' Stella, throughout the time I knew her, took a ridiculous number of supplements on top of Nurofen and an assortment of other headache tablets. Other people said that this had gone on for a large part of her life. All of a sudden, having left, she was able to stop taking all her supplements. Really? Where is the ownership of her issues, actions, and behaviours in saying or thinking this type of thing? Certainly not with herself! Crazy stuff.

'I won't be coming around with a mop and a bucket to clean up after you and your children.'

Once again, said to me by Stella not long after she left, implying that my children and I lived like pigs and were not going to look after the marital home, which was now something she saw as her investment property. An awful and tasteless thing to say and think. Only weeks before, she was the stepmother to my children. Now it seemed they meant next to nothing to her.

'I have worked very hard to re-establish my life in the last couple of months.'

This comment was made to me at the final dinner we had together that I ended up walking out off. I came to understand that this is a typical behaviour of a person who suffers from NPD. They simply move on when they have finished with a relationship, either on their terms or because they have been 'spotted' or called out for what they are by their unfortunate partner. Stella was no different. People are simply cut off, unfriended and blocked. It's time to start all over again and run the same template. People who suffer from NPD are accountable and responsible for nothing. It is simply not their fault, in any way.

'I have worked hard all my life. I have waited thirty years for my career to take off, and I am going to run with it.'

This comment was made just after our marriage ended. It shows that everything was all about Stella. Her career was taking off and was very exciting. It was giving her all the power, control, gifts, and gratitude that she needed, as an NPD sufferer. Her successes in the corporate world were giving her all she needed and boosting her sense of self. Her family, who had supported her and greatly assisted her in reaching this career high, had done their job. It was time to move on.

'You remind me of my father, you manipulative bastard.'

Just a classic comment from Stella. It occurred during a heated telephone conversation we had after our separation. I was being screamed at again, and giving back as good as I was getting. Seemingly, at a point where she lost control of what she was thinking and saying, this comment came out.

It was a real watershed moment for me. I stopped speaking upon hearing this and paused in complete silence. All of a sudden Stella, having realised what she had said, continued with words to the effect of, 'Don't go making up a story around what I just said.' She also told me not to consider that her relationship with her father was, 'part of some mental issue that you think I have.' I didn't reply, and remember a sense of calm coming over.

'Just like you're not accountable for being an absent husband who gave his wife fuck-all emotionally, other than lectures on how to be happy, and removed EVERY PIECE of accountability from yourself for how your actions impacted me!'

This comment, not surprisingly, also came after our marriage ended. It was an absolutely classic narcissistic thing to say. Her issues were simply being reflected onto me.

The reality was that *she* had significant psychological and emotional issues, and she did not take any personal accountability or responsibility for facing up to them. These issues were simply all my fault. I was far from an absent husband. She was the one travelling interstate two to three times a week, and was emotionally absent from our marriage. Trying to talk to Stella about her personal issues was taken as lecturing. As a loving and caring partner, trying to talk with Stella was my way of attempting to help her, and encouraging her to face up to her obvious psychological and emotional issues by implementing the help of a professional. What I was saying was simply too close to the truth. Everything was all about Stella.

She was a victim.

'You need to see a psychologist and ask them why you deliberately and intentionally did not look after any of my needs throughout the entire relationship.'

It was the question that I was directed to ask of my psychologist at my first session.

The Good Things That Happened

I think is it fair to say that very few of us are all bad. Stella was no different in this regard. We all have our good points.

It would be remiss of me not to briefly devote a section of the book to the good times I had with Stella. We did have some genuinely good times together.

Our courtship was near perfect and, with the benefit of hindsight, too good to be true. Stella was just about everything I wanted to find in a life partner. She was attractive, fun to be around, a professional woman who was relatively financially independent, a go-getter type who seemed like a hip-hop happening person. She seemed family orientated, a good mother, who was interested in my children and creating a long-term family environment. None of the negative actions and behaviours I have talked about throughout the book were evident, apart from the one minor occasion I have previously mentioned. I felt like a very lucky man indeed.

Once married, Stella completely changed. With all the good things that happened, there was an undertone of personal unhappiness about Stella that I was living with on a day-to-day basis. I was made to feel accountable and responsible for her. I also lived with the feeling that, from day one, Stella was emotionally absent from the marriage. She admitted that this was the case after our marriage ended. As hard as I tried there was nothing I could do or say that made Stella happy. I lived within an emotionally empty marriage, always second-guessing myself and, in Stella's mind, always having just let her down, being just about to let her down, or actually in the process of letting her down. Stella had no trust in me, no belief in my feelings, and no ability to give me the benefit of the doubt.

Within this context good things did happen.

We had a wonderful overseas holiday with all our children to a number of different countries. This holiday was a real learning experience for all our children.

There were also a number of well-planned and fun-filled domestic holidays that we seemed to enjoy as a family.

Stella was also a very good cook and provided wonderful family meals, when she took the time out from her busy work schedule to prepare our food. She introduced my children to a variety of different dishes, which was great for them. She was also houseproud and conscious of keeping a clean and tidy household.

I also credit Stella with giving my children some good fashion common sense.

Another good quality that Stella had was her passion for photography. She took many wonderful pictures of my children and of family occasions, which were highly valued.

The money we both earned, when combined, gave us a well-above average lifestyle, which was also much appreciated. We did not want for much.

The Final Analysis

The Age of Narcissism

Are we seeing an explosion of narcissism in our society in recent times?

Narcissism is a less extreme version of Narcissistic Personality Disorder. Narcissism involves cockiness, manipulation, selfishness, power motives, vanity, and a love of mirrors.

Narcissistic Personality Disorder is a mental disorder in which people have an inflated sense of their own importance, a deep need for admiration and a lack of empathy for others. But behind this mask of ultra-confidence lies a fragile self-esteem that's vulnerable to the slightest criticism.

The above definitions have been taken directly from the internet, from many and varied sources. They are an accurate description of Stella's actions and behaviours as experienced by me and, I understand, other partners.

My psychologist pointed out to me that the latest research findings, with reference to the Psychology Today website, conclude that narcissists do not have fragile self-esteem, and that the slightest criticisms of them may shatter the mask they hide behind, but not their egos.

I understand that up until quite recently psychologists accepted that narcissistic behaviour was a result of DNA, childhood upbringing and, for want of a better expression, the individual wiring of the brain. This wiring of the brain, that people with NPD have, as I understand it, can show up in brain scans. In recent times an acceptance has also begun to develop that people with NPD are, in fact, aware of what they are doing and choose to behave in this way.

It is my view that the increase in narcissistic behaviour in our society is a combination of many other things.

Firstly, I think it could be the result of an 'it's all about me' attitude that seems to run through our very entitled and disposable society. Children are taught from a young age that they have individual rights but are not taught that those rights come with associated accountabilities and responsibilities. If something goes wrong, then the attitude that it could not possibly have been their fault kicks in.

We seem to be promoting a namby-pamby, cotton wool world where everyone wins, and where we pander to our precious little petals instead of teaching them how to cope with the pressures of life. In many ways we have stopped real lessons being learnt. The reality is that life is not necessarily fair, not everyone wins, not everyone will stroke your little ego. If you are lucky enough to have choices, then decisions have to be made and, as a result, there are consequences. Each of us is responsible for our actions and behaviours.

Could a second reason be related to generations of dysfunctional families as a result of war? I am thinking here of World War I, World War II, the Korean War, the Vietnam War, and the many Middle East conflicts.

Maybe the rise of feminism and the need to 'keep up with the Joneses' has played a part, with more women in the workforce seeking career opportunities in preference to staying at home and raising their young children to at least school age. I am not being at all critical of the choices being made by females, just sharing a thought.

I believe one of the main causes is the rise in social media and online communication. They have allowed for a lack of responsibility in communication between human beings.

It was not all that long ago that, if you were in a room full of family, friends and other people, you were in the moment. These days, the ability to communicate with the whole world is also in the room with you, which leads to people judging themselves as to how they stack up against all manner of other people, situations, and circumstances.

I ask if this type of communication and validation of yourself is good, in the long term, for your sense of self-worth.

DNA or Environment?

My thoughts on why I think Stella developed NPD.

These are only my thoughts and opinions, as a result of having experienced what I now understand to have been a classical narcissistic relationship. My thoughts and opinions are not scientifically based, and I am in no way qualified as a psychologist.

I firmly believe that Stella's development of NPD is a factor of many issues.

The first issue is that it is DNA based. As I understand it, up until very recently this is what the mainstream psychology professional thought was the principal cause of people developing NPD.

I can clearly see this having occurred with Stella. Her family life, from what I observed and was told by others, seems to have been very dysfunctional. She grew up in a manipulative, controlling, and conditional environment, with physical discipline. This resulted in Stella's walls going up for self-protection, her conditional thinking, scorecard mentality, Stella hoops, Stella facts, her perfectionist and control freak outlooks, as well as a constant need to have her love tanks filled. No-one was to be trusted, believed in, or given the benefit of the doubt.

Although this was not the best I have come across to grow within, it is most certainly far from the worst. Stella was fed, clothed, educated, and had a warm bed.

Parents are your first educators. They give you the framework and building blocks that form the foundation of your beliefs and values. As a parent to multiple children, I think by far the majority of parents do their very best under the circumstances they have lived through to give their children the best they can. In the case of Stella's parents, I can only wonder what shaped them in their younger years.

As a result of all of this, I think Stella developed a warped sense of herself. She saw her male siblings as receiving preferential treatment, took it upon herself to work hard to extract herself from her environment and to make something of herself, and become very insular in terms of looking to rely on, trust, or truly befriend others. I strongly believe that Stella's childhood environment also stunted her emotional development.

Hugs and touch from her parents may have been at a premium, as well as the encouragement to develop a solid sense of self. Most importantly, the establishment of solid value and belief systems is highly likely to have not taken place.

The three or four times I saw Stella incredibly distressed and crying were manifestations of all of this. They were difficult moments to watch as a loving partner. To me, these incidents were like moments of reflection and insight into herself that Stella ultimately chose not to act upon. The choice she made was to do nothing. She did not face up to the psychological and emotional issues that she knew were there in order to be a far better person. Her choice was more denial, and the deflection of her unhappiness onto external factors and other people, such as me. I firmly believe that Stella's interpretation of her childhood is one of the leading factors that resulted in her developing NPD.

Whilst obviously not the best childhood, I have heard of far worse. Her interpretation of her childhood is significantly different and far less forgiving than that of her others siblings. In saying this I can understand how Stella developed strong defence mechanisms, which she still employed towards her parents, to protect herself from further pain. Her interactions with her parents seemed staged, managed, lacking in empathy, and disconnected. A lot of negative learned behaviours were involved in her interactions with her parents, which I and others could also see in the way Stella was raising her own children.

I tried to help Stella with all of this throughout the time we were together. Having experienced the type of unconditional love-based childhood that I had I really felt empathy for her, and naively wanted it all to change for Stella.

I talked to her about trying to change her relationship with both her parents, to do something different and take more control. The idea was to make peace with them both, for everyone's sake, or at least to make peace with them for herself. I tried to get Stella to see the good in them, and put away the bad in a place in her brain where it would not do her any more harm. It was all to no avail.

Perhaps a final comment here on Stella's interpretation of her childhood, which I came to understand was significantly different to her other siblings. I wonder if this interpretation also contributed to her developing NPD.

To me everyone has issues and challenges to face up to in life that can bring us to our knees. That's life. We can choose to ignore, deny, or deflect these issues. If we take this path, inevitably, things are highly likely to get worse. It is not the fact that we all have personal issues to deal with, it is the way you stand up to them, identify them, take ownership of them, move on from them, and do not let them define you that gives you your true character.

To her credit, Stella made a number of attempts to seek help, but retreated from the help when the same issues were identified time and time again by a host of professionals. She simply refused to face up to things, confront them, deal with them, get past them, and ultimately be a happier and far better person than the person she had made the choice to be. Fear won out every time.

One way to define insanity is 'doing the same thing over and over again and expecting a different outcome.' In the case of being involved in a relationship with an NPD sufferer, only the recipents of their actions and behaviours change. It is never the NPD sufferer's fault and they simply do not take responsibility or hold themselves accountable for the trail of emotional destruction they leave behind.

Another issue that I feel led to Stella developing NPD was the emotional turmoil that she lived with, as a result of her anxiety. Heightened anxiety is a hideous infliction to live with, and ultimately manifests itself in a range of physical symptoms. Severe anxiety is akin to an out-of-body experience, an intense battle between the rational mind and the irrational mind.

Stella was forever complaining about some physical issue. Headaches, backaches, neck aches, aching hips, leg and chest pains, insomnia, issues with her menstrual cycle and menopause, were constantly coming to the forefront of her thinking.

It was obvious to me that almost all of Stella's physical issues were due to her significant emotional and psychological issues, which she chose to ignore, manifesting themselves through her heightened anxiety. It was incredibly frustrating to watch and not be able to help.

I think another issue why Stella developed NPD is that she simply chose not to do anything about it. She had an awareness of her emotional and psychological issues, but made the choice not to act. This was to everyone's detriment.

From what I experienced and lived through, I think narcissists, up to a point, choose to live the way they do. You have to keep working on yourself in order to improve.

Stella did not like herself and the person she had become. She told me this on a number of occasions. She often used to express a desire to be famous, or to be good at something. Now that I am more educated on the subject of NPD, and the fact that narcissists see themselves as being better than others, I wonder if Stella's comments were nothing more than a prompt for me to praise her. In private, Stella appeared to be uncomfortable in her own skin. This may also have been an act or display.

I want to try and illustrate the previous point by talking about a concept that I have called 'the triangle.' This refers to my description of the relationship that I experienced with Stella after we married.

There was a constant and exhausting battle going on with Stella. This battle was between the person she portrayed herself as being, and her inner self. She took no responsibility whatsoever for these differences. Inwardly and privately she gave the impression that she did not like who she was and that her life wasn't perfect. This was blamed on external factors, particularly me. I was nothing more than a combatant to Stella.

However, the battle was not between me and Stella directly, but between Stella's inner and outer perceptions of herself, in combination with her grandiose expectations of how her life should be. All her negative issues were mirrored on to me. I was completely to blame and fully responsible for her unhappiness. Stella's battle both directly and indirectly involved me, which is why I have called it the triangle. It was as though I was the third party in the relationship. It is impossible to help someone who doesn't want to help themselves.

Stella was close to being a compulsive liar. She was not only lying to me in the way she acted and behaved and misrepresented herself, but also to our children, family, and friends. Most importantly she was lying to herself. The abrupt end of our marriage came as a considerable surprise to our children, family, and friends, because the act and display that Stella put on was so convincing. She often stated that my actions were not matching my words.

The only thing that Stella did where her words matched her actions was telling me she was moving out, ordering a removalist truck, and then actually leaving.

The Devil is in the Fine Print

My thoughts on what I think NPD is about.

Narcissists look the same as a normal person, but I am absolutely convinced their internal wiring is different. Although their brain may be structurally similar to a normal person, they run on their own power circuit with the way they think, act out, and behave. Every now and again there is a tantrum, emotional meltdown, tirade or issue, which is akin to a transformer on their circuit blowing up and then being in need of repair.

These people do not, or are unable to, connect with the larger grid, which contains normal people who have normal emotions and feeling towards others. The missing connection point for narcissists is empathy. This is the only thing they cannot fake or act out. Everything is all about them, always.

I understand and accept that we all put on an act to varying extents in our day-to-day dealings with people. With balanced and normal people this may be to accentuate a personal quality or contribute in a particular situation. It is about putting your best foot forward. The surface acting out does not run much deeper than that and, most definitely, does not compromise our sense of self.

With narcissists, this act runs much deeper. It is about elevating themselves in every situation possible. Recent research findings about narcissists concludes that they need to portray themselves as being superior to or better than others. This is not to make up for very poor self-concepts, but because they actually believe they are superior. In reality, they have little sense of self and the acting out ends up becoming a much larger part of who they are than with a normal person.

Narcissists are takers in a giver's disguise. By this, I mean that they give to people and situations with an expectation of getting something far greater in return. Their giving is done with an undertone of 'look at me, validate me and praise me.' Although they give to others, they do so with a need to have the receiver give something back that, in their eyes, is of at least the same value. They do not understand the thrill or pleasure in giving, doing, or gifting to others. I believe narcissist's behave in this way because it's all about them, the promotion of a self-image to others, and, most importantly, to themselves.

These behaviours are designed to make up for, and boost, their validation-hungry sense of self-worth, that often hides behind a confident facade. It gives them a sense of control and power over situations and people, and perhaps even an adrenaline rush. The gratitude that they force others to feel is elevating, and makes them feel superior and special.

So this is what I think NPD is in a nutshell:

It's all about power and control over people and situations.

Whatever you do in return, do not be seen to have given the narcissist something better in return than they gave to you. It will not be appreciated nor good for you.

The Benefit of Hindsight

My thoughts on what I could have done better.

With the benefit of hindsight and the knowledge I now have of NPD, I am not sure that I could have done much to help Stella. Perhaps if I had come to the understanding of Stella's NPD issues much earlier than I did I may have been able to save our marriage and family, as well as helping her in more appropriate ways. These thoughts are, perhaps, a waste of time. There is no point in me accepting responsibility for this failing if Stella was also not going to see the need for her to accept responsibility for her NPD actions and behaviours towards me, and see the need to seek professional help to change for the better.

The reality is that everyone has a story. We all make mistakes. Everyone also has issues and challenges. We all have the choice about whether or not to acknowledge the issues and challenges we have and work on them for the better. If you choose to ignore them or deflect your issues and challenges onto other people, the chances for meaningful personal growth, in particular with regard to emotional maturity, are highly likely to be curbed. If you choose to ignore or deflect your personal issues or challenges and not acknowledge and work on them it is highly likely that your issues and challenges will eventually come to define your life, but not in a good way.

Within three weeks of getting married I knew something was seriously wrong with our relationship, and that a considerable change had taken place. Stella claimed that I was the one who had changed, but this was simply not the case.

I have a strong, but not overbearing, personality. This may not have helped, as I didn't completely lose my sense of self in the face of the constant onslaught of Stella's narcissistic ways. While she could not completely control me she nearly destroyed me. I let this happen to me.

A close friend expressed the opinion that they thought I could have been a little softer with Stella at times, as I tried to help with her issues. I have to accept this view. Then again, I admit I had no idea what I was dealing with at the time. Perhaps I was too motivated by trying to help Stella.

I knew the problem and the solution lay within Stella. If Stella had decided to finally take ownership of her issues and seek the right professional advice and be willing to implement the advice on an ongoing basis, with my loving support, then she could have overcome her issues.

There was a constant theme in the message that I tried to convey to Stella and it was as follows:

You cannot be truly liked and loved by someone else, for simply being yourself, if you do not like and love yourself in the first place. In liking and loving yourself it doesn't mean that you need to have gone to the fullest extent of being a narcissist. You are also fully responsible for the way you see your inner self, your self-concept, values, and beliefs, including the way you project them to the world and people around you. If you like and love yourself, and are comfortable in your own skin without being a narcissist, then you will hopefully have the opportunity to meet someone who complements you, shares common interests with you, and is in the same space. A relationship that is meaningful and fulfilled will then have the opportunity to develop.

In conveying this message, I was genuinely trying to help Stella, but not knowing what I was dealing with. That is what a normal and loving partner would try to do. Maybe it was a male thing. Trying to fix things so we could move forward as a happily married couple. I fully accept that a person cannot help someone they love if that person doesn't see the need to be helped or doesn't want to be helped and supported in making the changes for themselves.

I most certainly wasn't trying to change Stella. Nobody has that right. I can accept that Stella, in her most narcissistic state of mind, conveniently let herself think that I was trying to change her. This was simply not the case. You can only love someone for who they are. Was that my mistake? Which person was Stella? I saw a beautiful person struggling to define herself, understand who she truly was, and develop solid values and beliefs to fall back upon in times of personal turmoil and doubt. Emotionally she was like a child, disordered and vulnerable, living in a middle-aged body.

Without doubt, I know I experienced a classical narcissistic relationship. This was professionally validated for me when my psychologist read out the article describing the three stages of a narcissistic relationship. The relief I felt when this article was read out to me was palpable. I could easily see that my relationship with Stella had three distinct phases, and that the failure of the relationship and marriage was not all about me.

With the help of my psychologist, I came to clearly see that my relationship and marriage to Stella was far from normal. I made a genuine commitment to Stella and fell in love with her, based upon the person I saw in the courtship phase of our relationship. I was completely fooled by this display and felt very foolish about it for some time after our marriage had failed. Put simply, my relationship with Stella was not about two people who came together, married and simply grew apart.

Although I did not initially know that I had entered into a classical narcissistic relationship, I played my part in enabling Stella's behaviour by not setting clear borders and boundaries. I should have called Stella out a long time before I did.

Some years after the failure of my marriage to Stella, I attended a talk by a well-known person who had experienced considerable adverse publicity as a result of committing a number of petty theft crimes due to their undiagnosed mental-health issues.

The person concerned spoke about receiving a letter from their long-term partner, which they initially took as being unrealistic and threatening. The letter spoke about being concerned about what they thought were their longstanding personal issues, as well as asking them in a sensitive way to gain awareness of how their actions were affecting their life. With some further discussion, the letter was taken as one of love and real concern and seen as a catalyst for change.

What followed was a period of professional help where the years of denial were dealt with, a program of help put in place, and some important life changes undertaken.

With regard to Stella, the concerns I raised in my letter to her were taken very negatively. I genuinely cared about Stella and wanted my letter to her to be our catalyst for change. For some time after our marriage failed I wondered if I could have done things differently, but trying to truly connect to a person who has a psychological and emotional disconnect with themselves is virtually impossible. Stella had no emotional stability or self-sufficiency. Providing these things was my role in the relationship, and made me feel emotionally drained, depleted, and cheated.

Books of this nature are stifled by the laws of defamation. I am very confident in saying that I was subjected to years of emotional, psychological, and, on one occasion, physical abuse in a classical narcissistic relationship. I believe I should have the right to speak the truth. People who have been subjected to classical narcissistic relationships should be able to be heard. I believe their stories need to be told, and other people need to be put on alert.

I hope my story helps people change their circumstances for the better. If it warns people away from entering a narcissistic relationship, helps someone identify that they are caught up in a narcissistic relationship, convinces someone to challenge their narcissistic partner, or to leave, move on from, or recover from a narcissistic relationship, then that would be the best possible outcome.

If these outcomes were achieved, then my time spent with Stella wouldn't amount to wasted years.

My experience with Stella saw me lose my faith in my own judgement for a while. There were some good times, but there was a constant undertone of being made to feel accountable for Stella's unhappiness. This feeling was extremely difficult to live with. I came to see and understand she was, in fact, projecting onto me.

Second-guessing myself and not trusting people as much as I had in the past were issues for a while. Despite being fully tested by the experience, the resilience and strong sense of self that my stable and loving childhood gave me, helped immeasurably with my recovery process.

I will always remember and take heart from my mother's words when my relationship with Stella inevitably ended. She said, 'Do not give too much of your time or pain to Stella now it is over. All you are doing, if you do, is wasting your emotional energy. Please do not become a bitter man. Thoughts of revenge are also a complete waste of time. Her pain may well be ongoing in choosing to live the way that she does. Imagine all the energy that goes into acting out, exaggerating, and overcompensating every aspect of her life on a daily basis. It is up to her to deal with her inner demons and get on top of them if she has the desire and willpower to do so and be the person she could be, if she did. You have done your very best to help her. It is not your problem to deal with anymore.'

The conclusion of my book changed significantly following a session I had with my psychologist as a result of her kindly agreeing to review my draft manuscript.

Up to this point in time my truth, interpretation, and acceptance of the experience with Stella had settled in my mind.

My truth has been described openly and honestly within this book. I have detailed my experience with Stella and discussed my views as to why there has been an explosion of narcissism in recent times, why I think Stella developed NPD, and what I think narcissism is about.

I have discussed my experience with Stella with the definition of narcissistic personality disorder (NPD) in mind.

I have also been open to looking at my experience with Stella with regard to the latest research into narcissism. This research, as I understand it, does not see NPD sufferers as having fragile self-esteem, but views them as incapable of feeling empathy. The research also shows that NPD sufferers have an awareness of what they are doing, and make a choice to live and behave in the way that they do.

As my story unfolded, I could easily identify with the previous and current views of NPD sufferers, in the experiences that I had with Stella, although I would still lean towards her having a low self-esteem and a poor sense of self. I accept this is in conflict with the latest research findings about NPD sufferers, which conclude that NPD sufferers do not have low self-esteem.

As a result of my upbringing with parents who loved me unconditionally, I always have empathy and compassion, and try to give people the benefit of the doubt. As Stella's loving partner it was natural for me to try and help her with the significant emotional and psychological issues she struggled to live with. The desire to help her to be happier within herself was sincere and genuine.

I now accept that my help would have been seen by Stella as an attempt to change her. I can see far more clearly now that she did not want to change or see the need to change. In her eyes, she didn't have any issues or problems.

I also accept that I failed to be shaped and manipulated into being someone that complied with Stella's perception of love. To this day I probably still feel empathy for Stella with the way she chooses to live, but perhaps not as much now, in light of what my psychologist said after reviewing my draft manuscript.

Reality Check

My thoughts on how I was deceived by a partner with NPD.

As with my psychologist's appraisal of my manuscript, I came to realise that the extent of Stella's deception, and her narcissistic behaviour, was far deeper than I had thought.

My psychologist pointed out many examples of narcissistic behaviour that I had unknowingly described in my manuscript. These included manipulation, enragement, gaslighting, enslavement, engulfment, exaggeration, ingratiation, entrapment, a complete lack of empathy, divide and conqueror tactics, threats, disempowering tactics, and coercing me into positions where I became subservient. In my psychologist's professional opinion, Stella may have been afflicted with traits of borderline personality disorder (BPD) as well as narcissistic personality disorder (NPD).

To my psychologist, Stella wore a false mask at all times, always working towards keeping reality at bay, and constantly engaging in games of cat and mouse. A 'push me away and pull me in' game was being played by Stella at all times.

The crying episodes that I thought were genuine, and Stella's expressions of low self-esteem and poor self-worth, were, in my psychologist's opinion, fake and false.

I was stunned by all of this.

With all of this professional confirmation of Stella's actions and behaviours towards me, the only conclusion I could reasonably come to was that Stella is an example of a classically narcissistic individual, a person who likes and loves themselves to the extreme, at the expense of having little, if any, empathy or sensitivity towards others.

I also now fully accept and understand that I experienced a classical narcissistic relationship, backed up by the knowledge that I can name with absolute clarity the dates the 'euphoria', 'destruction' and 'push the delete button' stages of our relationship started and ended.

In the end I expressed the view to my psychologist that I accepted and fully understood that Stella had effectively done me like a dinner. I was like a pig on a spit, being slow cooked to the point where I became the psychological and emotional equivalent of pulled pork.

Final Thoughts

My thoughts on what I can learn from this experience.

The best I can think now is that the truth lies somewhere between my truth and the reality expressed to me by my psychologist.

I am inclined to think that the view of my psychologist, with regard to Stella, is closer to the truth. Stella likes and loves herself to the extreme, is fully aware of her actions and behaviours towards others, and has little, if any, empathy or sensitivity to the plight of others. Everything is always all about her. Stella sees no need to change, and nothing will change except for the recipients of her actions and behaviours in the way she chooses to live her life.

Although I feel it is best for me that Stella is no longer in my life, I nevertheless sincerely wish her all the best, good health, and every happiness. Fully understanding what this experience was about, I have been able to forgive Stella for all the pain and suffering the experience caused me and my children. Forgiving allows you to release the build-up of inner tension within yourself. To not forgive is only to result in bitterness and a waste of your emotional energy. I doubt that I will ever be able to completely forget the experience. It will be stored away, where it can do no harm.

I also now understand that the extent of my initial downward spiral, which surprised me, was the result of a combination of many things, including being involved in another failed marriage as well as feeling very responsible for the unfortunate effect that this would have on all our children. A stable family environment for our children was very important to me. On a personal level I think my initial downward spiral was about coming to terms with the shock of realising the extent of Stella's deception and level of misrepresentation to lure me into our marriage during our courtship phase. This was very difficult to come to terms with, and very damaging to my sense of self, as I was forced to admit that I well and truly fell for it all.

I am somewhat of a fatalist. I believe that this experience, although extremely traumatising for me, has positively contributed towards the person I am today. I feel that my ability to write about it, as well as building the courage to publish it in order to try and help others who find themselves in similar circumstances, was meant to be. These types of experiences are life experiences and nothing is a disaster if you learn something from it.

I have found it quite interesting that a number of men and woman I spoke to have experienced similar narcissistic relationships. A common theme, amongst all of the people I spoke to, was that they'd had happy childhoods and upbringings. Is this why we were all so naïve in attracting our narcissistic partners, thinking we could fix things and stay by their sides until they saw the need to change for the better? Are they born this way? Is it as a result of life experiences lived? Perhaps a combination of the two? Do they see the need to change? Can they change or be helped to change? I have often pondered these questions, without coming up with definite answers.

Whether, knowingly or unknowingly, narcissists understand or care about the effects of their actions and behaviours on those with which they have personal relationships is, perhaps, a moot point. For someone on the outside, narcissists appear to live a life devoid of accountability and responsibility. They therefore act and behave in accordance with one rule only: What's in it for me?

Accordingly, they are never truly happy. There's always 'something wrong', and of course it's never them. I have therefore come to the conclusion that you can't please or appease people with NPD. Nothing short of a miracle will help or change them. Depending on the type of relationship you have with a narcissist, it's vital to your mental and physical wellbeing to protect yourself. Either by leaving them, avoiding them altogether, or keeping your distance or staying away from them as much as possible. In the end, it's self-preservation.

The level of Stella's narcissistic patterns of behaviour, I believe, was at the extreme end of the scale. I knew what a narcissist was, worked with many in my field of employment, but simply failed to see I had married one, until it was too late.

I have no issue with someone wanting to leave an unhappy relationship. The caveat is that a marriage should be entered into on a genuine basis and left after the very best attempts by those involved to save the relationship, especially if young children are involved. This would involve extensive relationship counselling, mature adult communication, and the clear explanation of the issues, and the solutions to those problems. None of this happened in our case. I wanted it to be adult-like, as I attempted to express in my final letter to Stella, but obviously failed.

Stella entered and left our marriage with no more than whimsical notions, demonstrating very capricious actions and behaviours. It is no wonder it failed.

My book is a long way from describing a normal relationship, where two people simply fall in and out of love. I naively thought we were two mature adults who both knew what we wanted.

Once we were married, Stella needed to have her understanding of love dominate our relationship. She had a need for power and control in order to feel validated. Her behaviour, including the crying episodes and regular tirades, were designed to elicit empathetic responses, but it was all very unbalanced, and terminal to our marriage.

To me, Stella had a situation-to-situation surface layer that ran far deeper than the norm. This deeper layer actually formed part of her sense of self. Power and control over people and situations defined her. Things she did for others came with an obligation to give back in a greater way or be and act in a way she wanted you to be or to act. The need for constant praise and self-gratification was her lifeblood. Nothing was undertaken or given by Stella unconditionally, to anyone. When you were finally manipulated into what you thought Stella wanted you to do or say, or for that matter not do or say, in order to keep the peace, it wasn't good enough. You simply couldn't win.

Living with Stella at the end of our marriage was surreal. It was like living in a fog. The only things that were clear was that there was nothing you could do or say that made her happy. It was as if what I thought was being directed at me, by Stella in private, through her actions, behaviours, vile tirades, and emotional absence from our marriage was exactly how she believed, in her mind, I was treating her. It was like a mirroring effect was taking place as well as maddening to both deal and live with let alone live within.

I accept full responsibly for being sucked in by Stella, all for her own good and self-promotion. I genuinely fell in love with her. I accept that the way I handled the experience effectively enabled Stella's behaviour. I did not set borders and boundaries that were acceptable to me.

It is also very important to me to acknowledge that the experience I lived through with Stella has made me the person I am today. There were some good times, particularly in the courting phase, and it was not all bad.

I am now very comfortable expressing the view that I have recovered and moved on from a classical, narcissistic relationship. Based upon the experience I have described in my book, the views of other people in my life, and the highly valued professional validation of my psychologist, I now understand and fully accept that, as a result of my experience with Stella, 'I Survived the Narcissist's Dance.'

Narcissist's Lament

If you are living a lie
looking into a mirror
It follows that you are lying to live
The mirror has no give
Caught between the perception and reality
of your true self
Managing layer upon layer
of how you see and want others to see yourself
Living in a potpourri of self-doubt
Not true to those of significance around you
as well as sadly yourself
Something will eventually give
It's no way to live.

Zac Thatcher